THEORY AND PRACTICE OF
MULTIPLE CRITERIA DECISION MAKING

THEORY AND PRACTICE OF MULTIPLE CRITERIA DECISION MAKING

Collection of papers presented at a workshop on
Multicriteria Decision Making
held in Moscow, May 1981

edited by

C. CARLSSON

Department of Business Administration
Åbo Academy, Åbo, Finland

and

Y. KOCHETKOV

International Research Institute on
Management Science
Moscow, USSR

N·H
P&C

1983

NORTH-HOLLAND PUBLISHING COMPANY – AMSTERDAM • NEW YORK • OXFORD

ISBN: 0 444 86579 9

Published by:
NORTH-HOLLAND PUBLISHING COMPANY
AMSTERDAM • OXFORD • NEW YORK

Sole distributors for the U.S.A. and Canada:
ELSEVIER SCIENCE PUBLISHING COMPANY, INC.
52 VANDERBILT AVENUE, NEW YORK, N.Y. 10017

Library of Congress Cataloging in Publication Data
Main entry under title:

Theory and practice of multiple criteria decision making.

1. Decision-making--Mathematical models--Congresses.
I. Carlsson, C. (Christer), 1946- . II. Kochetkov, Y. (Yevgeny), 1937- . III. Title: Multiple criteria decision making.
HD30.23.T44 1983 658.4'03 82-24873
ISBN 0-444-86579-9

EDITORS' PREFACE

This volume is part of a continuing scientific enterprise (or even adventure), which aims to compare achievements in management science within two different scientific traditions - western and eastern European management research. Contacts between different schools of thought are important because they offer opportunities for cross-fertilization of ideas, for exchange of experiences and for enhancement of understanding between researchers with similar interests but with different scientific backgrounds. The resulting synergy of scientific cooperation must be regarded as having a lasting, positive effect on international cooperation.

The papers published in this volume are developed and revised versions of papers originally presented at a seminar held in Moscow in May, 1981 by the International Research Institute of Management Sciences (IRIMS) and the Finnish Operations Research Society (FORS). IRIMS in Moscow offers a basis for joint research projects for management scientists from its sponsoring member-countries - Bulgaria, Cuba, Czechoslovakia, GDR, Hungary, Mongolia, Poland and USSR - and serves as a forum for scientific cooperation and exchange of research results in the management sciences. IRIMS organizes international seminars, sponsors and coordinates research projects, and publishes research reports.

The topic of the joint IRIMS-FORS seminar was Multiple-Criteria Decision-Making (MCDM). When preparing the seminar it evolved that it would be profitable to concentrate on one specific topic in order to bring methodological differences and similarities into focus. It also became clear that with a rather limited conceptual framework, obtained by concentrating on MCDM, we were able to communicate on a fairly non-abstract level. This offered possibilities for an exchange of experiences and ideas. A final motive for choosing MCDM as the topic was that this field offers new opportunities for management research, means and methods for more realistic problem-solving in a management context, and new challenges for the development of management sciences.

In the 1960's and early 70's the leading theme for theory development within management science was prescription: (i) identify and formulate a problem; (ii) create a model which is a valid and reliable representation of the problem; (iii) develop an algorithm which represents a rational way of approaching the problem; (iv) apply the algorithm to find an optimal solution to the problem; (v) prescribe the optimal solution as a norm for problem-solving and decision-making. The "rational way" is based on axioms and theorems representing ideal situations of rather an abstract kind; models are mathematical constructs to allow the use of mathematical algorithms, which are needed to find optimal solutions; model-users and problem-solvers should be fairly mathematically oriented in order to be able to use the models and/or the optimal solutions. Recent criticism of the prescription theme stresses that the results of modelling and problem-solving efforts may be invalid and useless if they are not built on an understanding of what a decision-maker does, why he is doing it and what he wants to do. In the 1980's we should therefore devote more attention to the decision process itself, try to understand its structure and dynamics and, as researchers, restrict ourselves to finding methods, means and techniques for supporting decision-makers. This task is more challenging than the previous prescription-oriented task because it requires that we work closer to the managerial context with all its imperfections and irregularities and that we gain a deeper insight into real-life decision processes. We believe that the experiences gained during the MCDM-seminar in Moscow will promote development towards a decision support methodology.

The papers included in this volume may tentatively be divided into three groups. The papers in the first group deal mainly with methodological problems.

The paper "Some features of a methodology for dealing with multiple-criteria problems" by C. Carlsson outlines some features of a methodology which we argue to be valid and useful for coming to terms with management problems, which are made complex by a requirement that multiple objectives should be attained. With multiple objectives follows a need to describe and evaluate a problem in multiple dimensions, to formulate and consider different aspects of it, and to assess their importance and relevance in some consistent way. These features add to the complexity of the class of problems dealt with. Complex problems are not uncommon in a management context although they may appear as fairly simple in various contexts: (i) when (over)simplified as a basis for problem-solving algorithms; (ii) when the essence of them is described by a seasoned and knowledgeable decision-maker; and (iii) when they are momentarily made simple because of some external influences. Even if they appear simple, these management problems need not be simple in fact, and there is some justification for developing a methodology for handling complex management problems; it is a way to more realistic problem-solving.

Here we will discuss three different approaches to such a methodology: (i) multiple-objective linear programming; (ii) fuzzy multiple-objective linear program-

MOLP

ming and (iii) a fuzzy systems approach. We will describe these approaches in some detail and find out to what extent they are valid and useful for handling management problems made complex by multiple objectives.

The paper "Fuzzy catastrophes in non-trivial decision making" by V.D. Dimitrov deals with the problems arising at the intersection of fuzzy set theory and catastrophe theory. The author uses a two-parameter fuzzy catastrophe to build up a model for generating non-trivial decisions. It is paper of theoretical character to a great extent.

In the paper "Complex ill-structured problems in management systems and their solution by man" S.V. Khaynish and A.G. Vlasov present a multi-stage procedure obtained by means of a descriptive approach to solve complex ill-structured problems. The procedure can be used to develop interactive systems which adapt to the actual problem-solver's behaviour both for the improvement of solution processes and the training of managers.

The second group of papers is devoted to methods for solving decision-making problems, with multiple criteria.

The paper "Some improvements to the Reference Point approach for dynamic MCLP" by M. Kallio and M. Soismaa deals with two improvements to the reference-point approach for trajectory optimization. First, a method to construct for each interactive iteration a feasible initial solution is presented. Its superiority in terms of CPU time to a straightforward approach of starting with a previous optimum basic solution is demonstrated with numerical experiments. Second, two approaches for smoothing optimal trajectories are presented. The first one employs adjustment via borrowing and saving whereas the second one restricts the objective to a linear combination of predetermined smooth trajectories. Numerical experiments with these two approaches are also presented.

The paper "Multiple-criteria optimization under uncertainty: concepts of optimality and sufficient conditions" by V.S. Molostvov is concerned with conceptual and technical problems arising in the field of optimization and game control with multi-valued objective functions. Applying the notions of extreme, saddle and equilibrium points to problems of this kind permits sufficient optimality conditions to be obtained.

The paper "SIMS, an interactive multicriteria search system" by O.A. Shestakov deals with problems of designing software tools that make it possible to use a large set of methods and procedures to solve practical problems of multicriteria search.

The paper "A sampling-search-clustering approach for solving scalar (local, global) and vector optimizing problems" by A. Törn is an approach for analysing objective functions under quite general conditions. The problems may either be constrained or unconstrained. The method does not put any restrictions on to the functional form of the objective function or the constraints. This means, for example, that the objective function could be multimodal and that the feasible region could be non-connected. The approach can also be extended to vector-valued objective functions. The basic ingredients used are multiple starting points, a local optimizer and a clustering analysis technigue, aiding in gaining efficiency and in displaying a global view of the problem analysed. The working of an algorithm implemented in Fortran is illustrated by some test problems. A nomography technique for visual presentation of the efficient solutions to MCDM problems is presented.

The third group of papers deals with applications of MCDM-methods for solving practical problems.

In the paper "Interactive systems resulting from a descriptive approach to the solution of complex ill-structured problems" by S.V. Khaynish and A.G. Vlasov the interactive systems DISIOR, DISIOR-RESOURCE and DISIOR-SPEKTR intended for solving complex ill-structured problems involving ordering the objects, resource allocation and planning respectively are considered. A detailed account of the second is given.

The paper "Multicriteria problems of sharing in pooling resources" by E.E. Dudnikov and V.S. Molostvov is also of applied character. The paper is concerned with optimization multicriteria models for establishing compromise variants of the contribution made by several interested parties to supplies of various resources for joint activities. These models are used for studies of a problem of pooling of resources in joint large scale CMEA construction projects.

As our editorial task is now completed we wish to extend our thanks for the authors for willing and enthusiastic work, to the referees from the EURO Working Group on MCDM for valuable advice and to the publisher for patience over and above the call of duty.

Christer Carlsson Y. Kochetkov

TABLE OF CONTENTS

THEORY AND PRACTICE OF
MULTIPLE CRITERIA DECISION MAKING
C. Carlsson and Y. Kochetkov (editors)

SOME FEATURES OF A METHODOLOGY FOR DEALING WITH MULTIPLE-CRITERIA PROBLEMS

CHRISTER CARLSSON

Department of Business Administration
Åbo Academy, Henriksgatan 7, 20500 Åbo 50, FINLAND

ABSTRACT

This paper outlines some features of a methodology which we argue to be valid and useful for coming to terms with management problems, which are made complex by a requirement that multiple objectives should be attained. With multiple objectives follows a need to describe and evaluate a problem in multiple dimensions, to formulate and consider different aspects of it, and to assess their importance and relevance in some consistent way. These features add to the complexity of the class of problems dealt with. Complex problems are not uncommon in a management context although they may appear fairly simple in various contexts: (i) when (over) simplified as a basis for problem solving algorithms; (ii) when the essence of them is described by a seasoned and knowledgeable decision maker; and (iii) when they are momentarily made simple because of some external influences. Even if they appear as simple, these management problems need not be simple in fact, and there is some justification for developing a methodology for handling complex management problems; it is a way to more realistic problem-solving.

Here we will discuss three different approaches to such a methodology: (i) multiple-objective linear programming; (ii) fuzzy multiple objective linear programming and (iii) a fuzzy systems approach. We will describe these approaches in some detail and find out to what extent they are valid and useful for handling management problems made complex by multiple objectives.

1. INTRODUCTION

In order to be able to make decisions under increasingly complex circumstances, I must evolve, maintain, and continually update a repertoire of views, values, opinions and convictions about the world. Such a personal "model" of reality provides the necessary navigational guidelines", the criteria which help to orient me as I face the ever-present dilemma of different possibilities of action ... Decision making is ultimately the most difficult (and potentially the most rewarding) activity because a "model" of any reasonable richness will return multiple criteria, forcing us to choose not only among the possible courses of action but also among the means of evaluating such actions. Milan Zeleny [59]

In order to create a sufficiently precise framework for our present endeavour, we will define "multiple-criteria decision-making" (MCDM) as the are area of decision-making which involves multiple attributes, objectives and goals. This definition is given by Zeleny, who defines its elements as follows (cf [59], pp 15-17):

"Attributes ... refers to descriptors of objective reality. They may be actual objective traits, or they may be subjectively assigned traits, but they are perceived as characteristics of objects in the 'outside'world.

Objectives are closely identifiable with a decision maker's needs and desires; they represent directions of improvement or preference along individual attributes or complexes of attributes.

Goals are fully identifiable with a decision maker's needs and desires. They are a priori determined, specific values or levels defined in terms of either attributes or objectives.

Criteria are measures, rules and standards that guide decision making. Since decision making is conducted by selecting or formulating different attributes, objectives or goals, all three categories can be referred to as criteria. That is, criteria are all those attributes, objectives or goals which have deen judged relevant in a given decision situation by a particular decision maker (individual or group)."

This definition of the MCDM-area is, of course, one of many possible, but it is composed of elements easily acceptable as key part of any decision problem. The elements form a basis for a further conceptualization of the area of interest.

Decision-making is selecting or choosing one alternative course of action from an existing relevant set of possible courses; decision-making requires that at least two criteria are present, otherwise no deliberate choice is needed and a mere creation of a means for measurement is sufficient for selecting an appropriate alternative course of action. "Decision-making" with only one criterion is a simple process of searching through unidimensional, finite set of action representations and selecting an alternative with the "best" value relative to the chosen dimension. With two or more criteria, however, it is necessary for a decision-maker (represented by a group or an individual) to consciously compare alternatives with the criteria, i.e. to define an order of priority between the criteria and to decide how the various dimensions should be related. Decision-making with two or more criteria should not be restricted by some given set of alternative courses of action, as the decision-making process may reveal, identify or create some alternative hitherto unknown or considered irrelevant. This means that the initially relevant alternative courses of action should be considered only a preliminary set, and the decision-making process should allow for extensions of that set. Let this be our first step in conceptualizing the MCDM-area.

Although theorists tend to make a distinction between planning and decision-making, managers themselves tend to regard the distinction as rather fuzzy, and like to point out (as some of my friends do) that adopting a plan is to decide on a set or a series of future actions. The distinction is often made as a basis for conceptualization, and we will draw upon a set of concepts (cf Anthony [2], pp 16-18):

"Strategic planning is the process of deciding on objectives of the organization, on changes in these objectives, on the resources used to attain these objectives, and on the policies that are to govern the acquisition, use and disposition of these resources."

"Management control is the process by which managers assure that resources are obtained and used effectively and efficiently in the accomplishment of the organization objectives."

"Operational control is the process of assuring that specific tasks are carried out effectively and efficiently."

These concepts identify three levels of decision-making activities: (i) a strategic, (ii) a management or tactical, and (iii) an operational level, and observe that the scope of the activities differs from level to level. In other words: MCDM may have different characteristics at different levels. Let this be our second step in conceptualizing the MCDM-area.

Decision-making activities are sometimes characterized as problem-solving processes, i.e. in such a way that the decision-making is facilitated when a problem is either solved or resolved. In the MCDM-area we talk about problems involving multiple criteria, which means that there are several goals or objectives to be attained, and it is not clear how that should be achieved - or that there are several attributes which represent unsatisfactory states, and it is not known how a change should be carried out. A problem is thus regarded as an identifiable entity, a selected area of action, for which a decison-maker (a group or an individual) is responsible. From a methodological point of view a problem-solving process is a well-defined activity (cf the problem-solving process of Operations Research); in a critical assessment Ackoff, however, wrote (cf [1], pp 237-239):

"... problems exist only as abstract subjective constructs, not as concrete objective states. Furthermore, I will argue that, even if they were objective states, they would not have solutions, if by 'solutions' we mean actions that extinguish a problem or put it to rest. I will maintain that in dealing with problems and solutions we have been dealing with shadows rather than substance."

An immediate reaction to this assessment is - "of course"; to formulate a problem is to introduce a conceptual basis for handling a situation of some concern to a decision-maker, and a conceptual basis may well be an abstract subjective construct. When solving a problem we are thus working with a simplified description of the real problem, and we hope to learn something useful for handling the real world situation. Thus we will take multiple-criteria problem-solving to be a part of the MCDM-area; let this be our <u>third</u> step in conceptualizing the MCDM-area.

In order to be able to deal with complex problems - problems related to multiple criteria often become complex because the criteria are interdependent - we have to introduce a simplified representation of them, i.e. descriptions which embrace only a few but essential aspects of the problems. As essential aspects we regard those features of a problem which are relevant and valid with respect to the multiple criteria. The process of constructing representations of a problem is known as modelling, for which we often develop a specific methodology (we have methodologies for analytic models, simulation models, etc).

Modelling may be classified according to three different levels of description in a management context: (i) the methodological level, (ii) the algorithmic level and (iii) the operational level, which differ from one another in terms of abstraction and the degree of detail of the concepts involved. Thus level (i) concepts have fewer details than level (iii) concepts, but they are more general and thus relevant to a wider context than level (iii) concepts, which are rich in detail but aimed at a limited context or area of interest. The realism of a model is dependent upon the purpose for which it is to be used: on level (i) its purpose is to provide insight into a context, on level (ii) to provide a basis for calculations, and on level (iii) to give some clues for action. As there is a certain parallelism between levels (i) -(iii), and the classification of decision-making activities at a strategic, a tactical and an operational level, we will make that parallelism explicit:
- level (i) models are useful representaions of strategic activities,
- level (ii) models may serve tactical activities, and
- level (iii) models should be useful for operational activities.

Linking the two categories is, admittedly, to simplify matters a bit: level (ii) models, for example, are useful also for operational and strategic activities. As our purpose is to work out some features of a methodology, the simplification appears to be rather useful: we will be able to reduce the complexity of the task somewhat. Then our fourth step in conceptualizing the MCDM-area is the observation that we can make use of models to facilitate multiple-criteria problem-solving and decision-making; we may distinguish "MCDM-models" of levels (i) - (iii).

Then to summarize our four steps, we may observe that they were intended as a means to conceptually delimitate the MCDM-area; this, in turn, forms the basis for a discussion of some features of a methodology for dealing with multiple-criteria problems. So far we have decided that MCDM is the area of decision-making which involves multiple attributes, objectives and goals; that initially relevant alternatives of action form a preliminary set, which should be extendable; that MCDM has different characteristics for different levels of decision-making activities; that multiple-criteria problem solving is part of the MCDM-area; and, finally, that models may facilitate multiple-criteria problem-solving and decision-making, and could be classified according to three different levels of description.

In the following we will briefly introduce a conceptual framework for a management context developed by Johnsen, and formulate a case example in order to make more precise the intuitive meaning of a decision problem with multiple criteria.

1.1 A Conceptual Description of a Management Context

Many of the elements we introduced in the previous section were used by Johnsen in 1975, cf [23] as parts of a conceptual framework for describing a management context. Johnsen's framework is constructed to support the managerial role as it is enulted by a manager; the context is formulated and discussed as it is seen through the eyes of a manager (cf [23] p 28; translated from Danish): "I want to study a context with the help of a specific model of the situation, and I want to communicate my insight into the situation through the terminology outlined by this model. I know what my objective is, and I select my means for attaining that objective on the basis of my perception of the situation at hand."

The objectives which the manager strives to attain may in Johnsen's classification belong to one of three categories:
- operational management, with relatively stable conditions,
- adaptive management, when conditons change and cannot be controlled, and
- management for development, when conditions change but can be influenced.

The means a manager could make use of in order to attain a goal are described as means for problem-solving; the means too are classified into three categories:

- analytical tools, which are used to identify and exploit cause-effect relationships,
- interactive methods, which rely on communicating with people, influencing their ways of behaviour and being influenced by them,
- search-learning methods, which combine the previous two categories such that a synthesis may be reached.

The language for communication, for formulating and testing means, and for expressing objectives, is the language of a theory of management. In Johnsen's classification there are, again, three categories of languages:

- decision analysis, and concepts derived from the analytical paradigm,
- behavioral science, and concepts derived from the behaviouristic paradigm,
- systems research, and concepts derived from the systems paradigm.

When the three classes of concepts are combined, we have the following three-dimensional construct (adapted from Johnsen, cf [23] p 25, fig. 1):

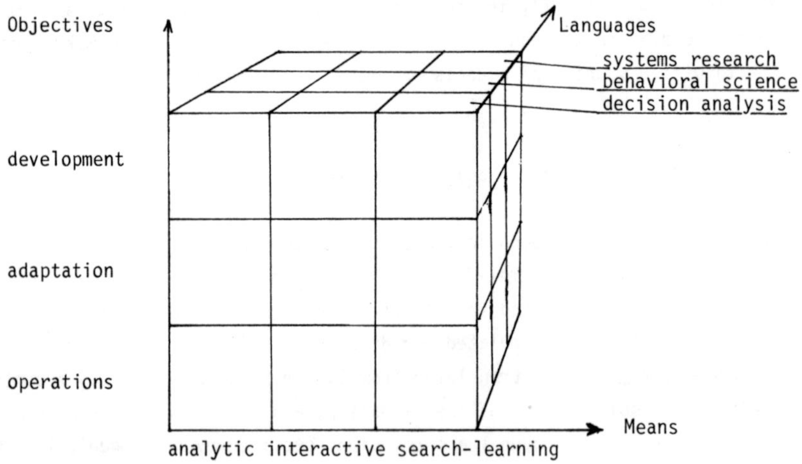

Fig. 1. Conceptual elements of a theory of management.

Combining the categories listed in fig. 1, we get 27 subcategories of elements, which now describe the theory of management more precisely: if we combine decision analysis - development objectives - search-learning means we get the "cube" for strategic decisions, for example. By working through the whole structure we will get a fairly exhaustive review of the management context; here, however, we will concentrate on only a few "cubes":

- decision analysis - operations objectives - analytic means
- systems research - adaptation objectives - analytic means
- systems research - development objectives - search-learning means

in order to find out how the MCDM-area should be conceptualized.

In the next section we will introduce a case example, which will serve as a basis for a description and discussion of the three "cubes" we have singled out.

1.2 Case Text

Our example is a typical case text in the sense that it has a real world basis in a Finnish company, but focuses on an abstract formulation of the problem situation we found to be important and interesting at one point of time. This means that we have concentrated on a few "essential" aspects and eliminated "superfluous" details. This was, of course, a series of subjective simplifications, which might have turned out another way with another set of information. The aspects deemed essential at one point of time may, in retrospect and when we know the results of our decision, appear to be less essential; the point is, however, that a necessary condition for retrospective learning to occur is that we have carried out the modelling and problem-solving process and found out if, and how well, it works.

The company has an annual turnover of about 600 Mmk, but is one of the smaller companies in the Finnish timber industry. It is divisionalised, and has divisions for (i) paper and pulp, (ii) plywood, (iii) chipboard, (iv) sawn timber and (v) shipping. Planning is organized in (i) rolling, 5-year strategic plans, (ii) 1-year, tactical plans and (iii) quarterly, operational plans. It is recognized that tactical plans have to be coordinated in such a way that the chief executive officer (CEO) is able to control all his divisions and to create and follow up overall policies for the company. It is also recognized that the interplay between tactical and strategic plans, and between tactical and operational plans, must be taken care of in some systematic and orderly fashion. Finally, it is also recognized that in a progressively growing company there must be both goal conflicts between the divisions, and shorter-term conflicts among the objectives implemented in tactical and operational plans, which must be dealt with in some rational way.

One year ago, during the strategic planning process, the CEO decided it was time to develop the planning process a bit, to create a systematic planning structure of strategic, tactical and operational plans - even perhaps to create a hierarchy of plans - and to build the whole system in such a way that it could be made operational in reality, not only in a theoretical framework. The CEO pointed out some obstacles that should be dealt with:

(1.1) there are n_i objectives for division i ($n_i > 2$, $i \in [1,5]$) which should be attained within the scope of a tactical plan - it is not clear how;

(1.2) the $\sum_i n_i$ objectives should be evaluated and assessed in the light of the strategic plan and the CEO's options for an overall policy - it is not clear if that is possible;

(1.3) he wants a scheme for assessing the relevance and relative importance of divisional objectives - it is not clear how such a scheme should be constructed;

(1.4) divisional objectives are interdependent: conflicts should be resolved or absorbed, supporting interdependences should be exploited - it is not clear if that is even theoretically possible;

(1.5) there may be degrees of attainment for the objectives, so that it is not quite clear if an objective is attained or not; the attainment of the objectives should, nevertheless, be compared and evaluated against different options for an overall policy - it is not clear if that is even theoretically possible;

The obstacles belong to the MCDM-area according to our four-step conceptualization of that area, and we will treat them with MCDM-tools in order to find out how well these tools apply - on a theoretical and methodological level.

Let A_1 - A_5 be multidimensional, multiple-attribute sets of alternative courses of actions relating to the five divisions; let G_0 - G_8 be multidimensional, multiple-attribute sets of objectives adopted by the five divisions. Then an extremely simplified, highly aggregated and abstract representation of the CEO's planning problem could be constructed as in fig. 2a - c: the dotted lines (---) indicate conflicts, the lines (———) supportive interdependences; the sets of objectives may be implemented exclusively for one A_i, or be shared by two or more divisions, resulting in a fairly complex structure.

Fig. 2 gives an intuitive description of the complexity involved in the type of planning situation we shall discuss. In the following we will find out how three different MCDM-approaches will succeed in tackling the complex we have in fig. 2(c): the multiple-objective linear-programming approach in section 2; the fuzzy multiple-objective linear-programming approach in section 3; and a systems approach in section 4. Our results are summarized and evaluated in section 5.

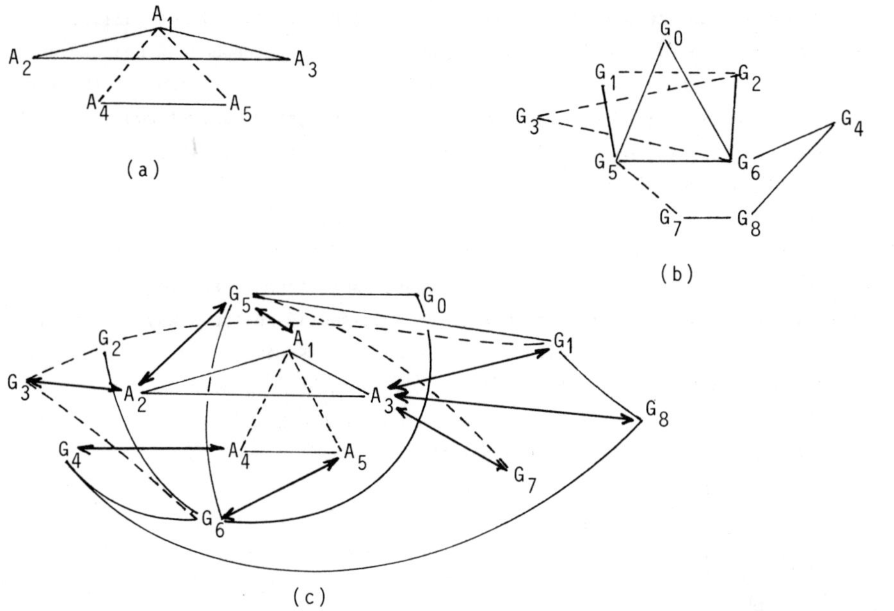

Fig. 2. (a) sets of alternative courses of action; (b) sets of objectives; (c) a complex of alternative courses of action and objectives.

2. MULTIPLE-OBJECTIVE LINEAR-PROGRAMMING

The multiple-objective linear-programming (or MOLP-) approach is a level (ii) modelling approach, which may also be used for level (iii) modelling. In Johnsen's scheme it may be described with the "cube" for decision analysis - operations objectives - analytic means, or possibly - adaptation objectives - as we shall find out. There are several contributions to the MOLP-approach (cf [3] , [8] ,[16] ,[22] , [25] , [51]), but here we will draw upon some previous work (cf [8] , [12]) in order to get a fairly brief description of some essential features of the technique.

We will use the case formulated in the previous section as a frame-work and background - with some slight simplifications: instead of dealing with all of A_1 - A_5, we will single out A_1 and A_2 and treat them as tactical plans for divisions 1 and 2; we will also use the set A_3, but take that to be a coordinutive plan at the strategic level - the difference in level is indicated by the indexes (h) and (h+1).

In this way we want to pinpoint one aspect of the problem situation outlined in the case text: the evaluation and assessment of many interdependent objectives in the light of a higher level (strategic) plan, which is a key element in the first three obstacles indicated in the case text. The discussion can, of course, be extended to all the sets $A_1 - A_5$, to more levels than (h) and (h+1): the extension is straight-forward.

If it is possible, in principle, to formulate a MCDM problem in theoretical terms the remaining, perhaps non-trivial task, is to find a way to solve the problem thus formulated. To this end we will in this section discuss ways of finding a composite optimal solution, i.e., a solution that is simultaneously optimal for all the three planning problems $A_1^{(h)}$, $A_2^{(h)}$, and $A_3^{(h+1)}$.

Let X, Y, and Z be convex hulls defined by

$$
\begin{aligned}
X &= \{ x \in \mathbb{R}^{n3} \mid A_3 x < B_3, x > 0 \}, \\
&\quad \text{where } B_3 \in \mathbb{R}^{m3} \text{ and } A_3 \text{ is an } m_3 \times n_3 \text{ matrix}, \\
Y &= \{ y \in \mathbb{R}^{n1} \mid A_1 y < B_1, y > 0 \}, \\
&\quad \text{where } B_1 \in \mathbb{R}^{m1} \text{ and } A_1 \text{ is an } m_1 \times n_1 \text{ matrix}, \\
Z &= \{ z \in \mathbb{R}^{n2} \mid A_2 z < B_2, x \quad 0 \}, \\
&\quad \text{where } B_2 \in \mathbb{R}^{m2} \text{ and } A_2 \text{ is an } m_2 \times n_2 \text{ matrix},
\end{aligned}
\tag{2.1}
$$

and let them represent fixed, non-empty regions extracted from $A_1^{(h)}$, $A_2^{(h)}$ and $A_3^{(h+1)}$ (i.e., $X \sqsubseteq A_3^{(h+1)}$, $Y \sqsubset A_1^{(h)}$, $Z \sqsubseteq A_2^{(h)}$. If we formulate

- alternative courses of action as time-independent one-dimensional variables
- interdependences as deterministic and linear equalities ,
- objectives as objective functions, in which coefficient vectors represent contributions of the alternative courses of action to corresponding objectives, or
- objectives as constraint levels, to be imposed on corresponding and relevant alternative courses of action.

If we, furthermore, - for a moment - disregard the possibility that the problems are interrelated, i.e., they form aggregates or parts of each other, it is possible to capture each of the problems $A_1^{(h)}$, $A_2^{(h)}$, and $A_3^{(h+1)}$ in mathematical programming models (s.t. means subject to):

$$
\begin{aligned}
MP_1 :\ & \max\ cy \\
& \text{s.t. } A_1 y - F^+ + F^- = B_1 \\
& y,\ F^+,\ F^- \geq 0
\end{aligned} \tag{2.2}
$$

$$
\begin{aligned}
MP_2 :\ & \max\ dz \\
& \text{s.t. } A_2 z - G^+ + G^- = B_2 \\
& z,\ G^+,\ G^- \geq 0
\end{aligned} \tag{2.3}
$$

where MP_1 and MP_2 are formulated in regions Y and Z and are assumed to capture all essential objectives and actions and their corresponding interdependences, of the original problems $A_1^{(h)}$ and $A_2^{(h)}$. Then to the higher level problem $A_3^{(h+1)}$:

$$
\begin{aligned}
MP_3 :\ & \max\ ex \\
& \max\ fw \\
& \min\ (R_1 F_1^+,\ R_2 F_1^-,\ R_3 G_1^+,\ R_4 G_1^-) \\
& \text{s.t. } A_3 x - F_1^+ + F_1^- - G_1^+ + G_1^- = B_{31} \\
& \qquad A_3' x + A_4' w \leq B_{32} \\
& \qquad A_4 w \leq B_4 \\
& \qquad x,\ w,\ F_1^+,\ F_1^-,\ G_1^+,\ G_1^-, \geq 0, \\
& \qquad \text{and } B_3 \ni B_{31},\ B_{32}.
\end{aligned} \tag{2.4}
$$

where MP_3 is a combined linear and goal programming model, formulated in regions X and W, (W is assumed to be a convex hull) where $W = \ w \in \mathbb{R}^{n4} \mid A_4 w \leq B_4,\ w \geq 0$, $W \sqsubseteq A_3^{(h+1)}$ and $B_4 \in \mathbb{R}^{m4}$ so that A_4 is an $m_4 \times n_4$ matrix; A_3' and A_4' are "appropriate" submatrices of A_3 and A_4. The first objective function and the first constraint are linked to MP_1 and MP_2 through the deviations captured in the F_1 and G_1 vectors (which are transformations to the X-region: $F_1 = \gamma_1 F$ and $G_1 = \gamma_2 G$) (2.1)-(2.4). The vectors of slack and surplus variables of MP_1 and MP_2 are thus reinterpreted as deviations from preset goals (cf. the goal programming formulations). The second objective function and the second constraint represent independent goals, which are assumed to be "composed" of the goals represented in MP_1 and MP_2 (cf. a comparison of two sets of goals in a common measure); the third objective function is a goal programming formulation in which all deviations from the constraints are minimized (R_1-R_4 are dimensionless preemptive weights).

Then MP_3 is rather a special and complex model: it is a multiobjective goal and a linear-programming model. We will try to find, and formulate, necessary and sufficient requirements for the existence of a composite optimal solution in the model, and also interpret the operational meaning of such a solution. For that purpose we will adopt the following strategy:

(2.5i) determine necessary and sufficient requirements for the existence of a solution to the goal programming part of (2.4.), i.e., the third objective function,

(2.5ii) identify the solution space for the goal programming solution,

(2.5iii) determine the set of non-dominated points within that space which solves the multiobjective linear-programming part of (2.4), i.e., the first two objective functions,

(2.5iv) by choosing one subset of non-dominated points, and applying some appropriate decomposition scheme, determine necessary and sufficient requirements for the existence of simultaneously optimal solutions to MP_1, MP_2, MP_3.

This strategy is admittedly of rather an heuristic nature - for specific problems there may exist more efficient solution procedures - but should suffice for our present purposes, i.e., it should help us find out both the existence and the nature of a composite optimal solution.

Then the goal programming (GP) part of (2.4) is given by $\min(R_1F_1^+, R_2F_1^-, R_3G_1^+, R_4G_1^-)$

$$\text{s.t. } A_3x - F_1^+ + F_1^- - G_1^+ + G_1^- = B_{31} \tag{2.6}$$

Let us assume that (2.4) has, or can be reformulated in, the following block structure (Fig. 3).

i.e., we can identify two parts of the x-vector: x which "represents" the Y-region and x' which "represents" the Z-region. Then it is possible to rewrite (2.6) in the following form:

$$\min \sum_{j=1}^{k} \delta_j \mid x_j - g_j \mid + \sum_{j=k+1}^{n_3} \delta_j \mid x_j' - g_j \mid$$

$$\text{s.t. } A_3^{(1)}x + A_3^{(2)}x' - G = B_{31}, \tag{2.7}$$

where $x, x' \in X$ and $g_j \in G$. Here we should further have $g_{ij} \in g_j (i = 1, \ldots, m_3)$ where the elements of the vectors are defined by

$$g_{ij} = \beta^{(1)}_{ij}F^{+}_{1i} + \beta^{(2)}_{ij}F^{-}_{1i}, \qquad \text{if } j = 1, \ldots, k$$

$$g_{ij} = \beta^{(1)}_{ij}G^{+}_{1i} + \beta^{(2)}_{ij}G^{-}_{1i}, \qquad \text{if } j = k - 1, \ldots, n_3 \tag{2.8}$$

so that,

$$\beta^{(1)}_{ij} = \alpha^{(1)} a_{ij} \sum_{j1} a_{j1}$$

$$\beta^{(2)}_{ij} = \alpha^{(2)} a_{ij} \sum_{j1} a_{j1},$$

for all j_1 (except j) in $[1, k]$ and $[k - 1, n_3]$, and $a_{ij} \in A^{(1)}_3$ or $\in A^{(2)}_3$ respectively. (2.9)

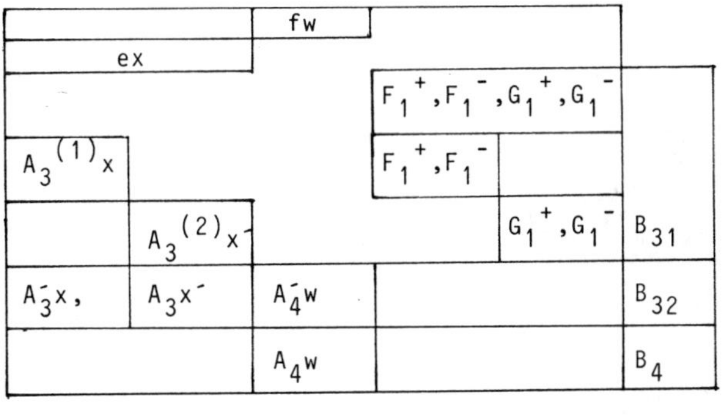

Fig. 3. The block structure of (2.4).

We should, furthermore, have $\alpha^{(1)}, \alpha^{(2)} \in [0, 1]$ so that $\alpha^{(1)} + \alpha^{(2)} = 1$, which offers a possibility for giving subjective weights to positive and negative deviations (here we will assume that $\alpha^{(1)} = \alpha^{(2)} = .5$, or $\alpha^{(1)} = 0$, $\alpha^{(2)} = 1$). Then it would be permissible to replace R_1-R_4 with δ_j and δ_i if we have $\delta_1 > \delta_2 > \ldots > \delta_k > \delta_{k+1} > \ldots > \delta_{n3}$; this ordering is arbitrary - if we for some reason should have $\delta_{n_3} > \delta_k$ we could just "reshuffle" the objective function.

If the goal-programming model is formulated as in (2.7)-(2.9) we can apply a general reduction lemma introduced by Charnes-Cooper et al.[15]; (2.7) is a linear convex goal functional and it should furthermore be possible to define limits for all the elements of x_j and x'_j

$$\bar{\varepsilon}_j^{(1)} < x_j,\ x'_j \leq \bar{\varepsilon}_j^{(2)}, \qquad \text{for } j = 1, \ldots, n_3. \tag{2.10}$$

Then the Charnes-Cooper lemma states that, if an x satisfies (2.7) and (2.10) and for some i_0, $x_{j0} > g_{j0}$, then x satisfies (2.7) and (2.10), and $f(\bar{x}) \leq f(x)$, where

$$\bar{x} \equiv (\ldots\bar{x}_j\ldots)$$
$$\bar{x}_j = x_j,\ j \neq j_0$$
$$\varepsilon = \max\ (\bar{\varepsilon}_{j0}^{(1)},\ g_{j0}).$$

Because of this lemma we can add one condition to (2.10):

$$x_j,\ x'_j \leq \max\ (g_j,\ \bar{\varepsilon}_j^{(1)}) \equiv \bar{\varepsilon}_j^{(2)} \tag{2.11}$$

and through this condition we now have $x_j - g_j \leq 0, \forall_j$ which implies that $|x_j - g_j| = g_j - x_j$; and correspondingly for x'_j. Then we can replace (2.7) by

$$\max \left(\sum_{j=1}^{k} \delta_j x_j + \sum_{j=k+1}^{n_3} \delta_j x'_j \right)$$
$$\text{s.t. } A_3^{(1)} x + A_3^{(2)} x' \leq B_{31} \text{ and}$$
$$\bar{\varepsilon}_j^{(1)} \leq x_j,\ x'_j \leq \bar{\varepsilon}_j^{(2)}, \forall_j . \tag{2.12}$$

Here (2.12) is an ordinary linear programming problem with a dual of the following form (which, however, is not the dual of the original goal-programming problem [16])

$$\min \left(vB_{31} + \sum_{j=1}^{n_3} (u_j^{(1)+} \bar{\varepsilon}_j^{(2)} - u_j^{(1)-} \bar{\varepsilon}_j^{(1)}) \right)$$
$$\text{s.t. } A_3^T v + u_j^{(1)+} - u_j^{(1)-} = \delta_j, \qquad j = 1, \ldots, n_3$$
$$v,\ u_j^{(1)+},\ u_j^{(1)-} \geq 0 \tag{2.13}$$

where A_3^T is the transpose matrix of $A_3^{(1)}$ and $A_3^{(2)}$, and v is the dual vector associated with x, x'. If we can assume that $\sum_j \bar{\varepsilon}_j^{(1)} \leq B_{31}$ (and this should be a save assumption as each $\bar{\varepsilon}^{(1)}$ represents a lower limit), then the optimal solution of (2.12) is

$$\overset{*}{x}_{j1} = \varepsilon_{j1}^{(2)} \qquad j_1 = 1, \ldots, m_1 - 1$$

$$\overset{*}{x}_{m1} = B_{31} - \sum_{j1} \varepsilon_{j_1}^{(2)} - \sum_{j_2} \varepsilon_{j_2}^{(1)} ,$$

where the summation is for $j_1 = 1, \ldots, m_1 - 1$
and $j_2 = m_1 + 1, \ldots, n_3$

$$\overset{*}{x}_{j_2} = \varepsilon_{j_2}^{(1)} , \qquad j_2 = m_1 + 1, \ldots, n_3 \tag{2.14}$$

as shown in [16], where the proof of the optimality is carried out through the dual formulation.

It should be observed that (2.14) is derived from the so called shadow costs of (2.13), which when reformulated in terms of x_j give (2.14), i.e., the optimal solution to the goal-programming part of (2.4).

Let us now consider the multiobjective linear programming (MOLP) part of (2.4). Following Kornbluth [25] we will introduce the concept of an efficient (Pareto-optimal, non-dominated) solution: a solution $x \in X$, $w \in W$ (to the MOLP part) is <u>efficient</u> if there are no other points $x' \in X$, $w' \in W$ such that

$ex' \geq ex$

$fw' \geq fw$, and

$ex' > ex$ or $fw' > fw$,

for at least one element of x' or w' . (2.15)

Here we will undertake the task of determining a set of properly efficient MOLP solutions by applying Kornbluth's methods to the first two objective functions and the restrictions of (2.4) - disregarding, for the moment, the vectors F_1^+, F_1^-, G_1^+, and G_1^- and using $A_3x < B_{31}$ as a constraint. After that we will determine necessary and sufficient requirements for the existence of solutions which are non-dominated in both the GP and the MOLP parts, and also find out if a solution could be optimal in both parts of the problem.

The problem we should solve is of the following form:

$$\begin{aligned} &\overline{\text{eff}}\ (ex,\ fw) \\ &\text{s.t. } A_3x \lesssim B_{31} \\ &A_3'x + A_4'w \lesssim B_{32}, \\ &A_4w \lesssim B_4 \end{aligned} \tag{2.16}$$

where $\overline{\text{eff}}$ denotes the problem of finding an efficient point in the vextor maximizing sense; here the vextor x contains both x and x' of the previous discussion. It has been proved, by Philip [36], that if there exists weights $\lambda_1, \lambda_2 \geq 0$ and $\lambda_1 + \lambda_2 = 1$, and if $\overset{*}{x}, \overset{*}{w}$ solve a problem of the following type,

$$\begin{aligned} &\max\ h(x,\ w) = \lambda_1 ex + \lambda_2 fw \\ &\text{s.t. } A_3x \lesssim B_{31} \\ &A_3'y + A_4'w \lesssim B_{32} \\ &A_4w \lesssim B_4 \end{aligned} \tag{2.17}$$

then $\overset{*}{y}, \overset{*}{w}$ also solve (2.16). In order to introduce necessary restrictions on λ we will have to apply the concept of a <u>properly efficient solution</u> (cf. Geoffrion [20]); an efficient solution $\overset{*}{y}, \overset{*}{w}$ is properly efficient if there exists a scalar $M > 0$, such that for each i, we have

$$\frac{h_i(x,\ w) - h_i(\overset{*}{x},\ \overset{*}{w})}{h_j(\overset{*}{x},\ \overset{*}{w}) - h_j(x,\ w)} \lesssim M \tag{2.18}$$

for some j such that $h_j(x,\ w) < h_j(\overset{*}{x},\ \overset{*}{w})$ whenever $x \in X$, $w \in W$ and $h_i(x,\ w) > h_i(\overset{*}{x},\ \overset{*}{w})$. According to a proof by Geoffrion [20], x and w are properly efficient to $\overline{\text{eff}}$ (ex, fw), $x \in X$ and $w \in W$ iff $\exists\, \overset{*}{\lambda}_1, \overset{*}{\lambda}_2 > 0$ and $\overset{*}{\lambda}_1 + \overset{*}{\lambda}_2 = 1$ so that $(\overset{*}{x}, \overset{*}{w})$ is optimal for $\overset{*}{\lambda}_1 ex + \overset{*}{\lambda}_2 fw$. On the basis of this result, Kornbluth [25] proves a duality theorem which is useful for our present purposes.

Given some weights $\overset{*}{\mu}$, $(\overset{*}{y}, \overset{*}{w})$ is properly efficient for the (primal) problem

$$\begin{aligned} &\overline{\text{eff}}\ (ex,\ fw) \\ &\text{s.t. } A_3x \lesssim B_{31}\overset{*}{\mu}_1 \\ &A_3'x + A_4'w \lesssim B_{32}\overset{*}{\mu}_2 \end{aligned}$$

$$A_4 w \le B_4 \overset{*}{\mu}_3$$

$$x,\ w,\ \mu \ge 0, \text{ and } \mu_1 + \mu_2 + \mu_3 = 1 \tag{2.19}$$

if and only if there exist a series of weights $\overset{*}{\lambda}$ and a vector of dual variables $(\overset{*}{s}, \overset{*}{u}, \overset{*}{v})$ such that $(\overset{*}{s}, \overset{*}{u}, \overset{*}{v})$ is properly efficient for the (dual) problem:

$$\underline{\text{eff}}\ (sB_{31},\ uB_{32},\ vB_4)$$

$$\text{s.t.} \quad sA_3^T \ge \overset{*}{\lambda}_1 e$$

$$u(A_3'^T + A_4'^T) \ge \overset{*}{\lambda}_2 (e + f)$$

$$vA_4^T \ge \overset{*}{\lambda}_3 f\ . \tag{2.20}$$

Then for every efficient (non-dominated) solution $(\overset{*}{y}, \overset{*}{w})$ of (2.16) we would have vectors of prices $(\overset{*}{s}, \overset{*}{u}, \overset{*}{v})$ which give a vector minimum for the values attached to B_{31}, B_{32} and B_4 by a decisionmaker.

Then it can be shown [25] that there are some restrictions $\overset{*}{\lambda}, \overset{*}{\mu}$ and $(\overset{*}{s}, \overset{*}{u}, \overset{*}{v})$ should satisfy: these are the Kuhn-Tucker conditions for the optimizing problems which result when the weights $\overset{*}{\lambda}$, $\overset{*}{\mu}$ are applied to form weighted objective functions in (2.19) and (2.20) (this is part of Kornbluth's proof).

Let $\overset{*}{x}_G$ denote the optimal solution to the GP part of (2.4), and let $(\overset{*}{x}_M, \overset{*}{w}_M)$ be the optimal solution to the MOLP part of (2.4); these solutions correspond to (2.14).

On the part of $(\overset{*}{x}_M, \overset{*}{w}_M)$ we should observe that it represents an extreme point in a set of non-dominated points (cf Yu-Zeleny [50]). Let X_M, W_M be the corresponding sets of non-dominated (Pareto-optimal or efficient) points.

Then remains to find out if $\overset{*}{x}_G$ is an extreme point in a set of non-dominated points; this is a trivial problem as there is only one non-dominated point in (2.7) and that is the extreme point $\overset{*}{x}_G$.

As non-dominated points are found in the corners and on the edges of a convex hull, and X and W were assumed to be convex hulls, let the corresponding (interesting) regions be

$$X_G = \{ x \mid A_3^{(1)} x + A_3^{(2)} x' - G = B_{31},\ |\bar{x}_j - \bar{g}_j| = \xi_j \qquad \text{for } j = i, \ldots, k \}$$

where $k < n_3$ (cf (2.7)) and $\varepsilon_j = 0$

for $j = 1, \ldots, k'$.

where $k' \leqslant k$.

$X_M = \{x \mid x$ are properly efficient for (2.19)$\}$

$W_M = \{w \mid w$ are properly efficient for (2.19)$\}$. (2.21)

Then our next problem is to find out if it is possible to get a combined optimal solution, i.e., solution vectors $\overset{*}{x}_G$ and $(\overset{*}{x}_M, \overset{*}{w}_M)$ where $\overset{*}{x}_G = \overset{*}{x}_M$. It should be observed that $\overset{*}{w}_M$ has a decisive influence on the existence of a combined optimal solution because of the common constraints shown in Fig. 3. We might even have to choose between $\overset{*}{w}_M$ and a combined optimal solution; here we will - for simplicity - assume that $\overset{*}{w}_M$ has some "appropriate" value. There seem to be four different cases of interest to be considered:

(2.22i) $X_M \sqsubset X_G$, due to the "common" constraints of x and w (cf. Fig. 3)

(2.22ii) $X_M \sqsubseteq X_G$

(2.22iii) $X_M \not\sqsubseteq X_G$ but $X_M \sqcap X_G \neq \emptyset$

(2.22iv) X_M / X_G and $X_M \sqcap X_G = \emptyset$. Here the two regions do not have any point in common; this could happen for example after a few steps in the process of solving the GP part of (2.4).

There are several and different solving procedures for tackling these four cases reported in the literature; we will just mention a few of them - interested readers are referred to original publications.

Let us assume that $\overset{*}{x}_G$ is represented by a point (a) and $\overset{*}{x}_M$ by either point (a') or (b').

Re 2.22i): If the constraints of the MOLP part of (2.4) cannot be changed there is clearly no combined optimal solution for the two parts in this case. In order to reach a combined (suboptimal) solution some of the goal attainment should be reduced in the GP part, for example by checking out the non-dominated points of X_M as solution proposals in the GP part (by the Charnes-Cooper formulation [15] and selecting a$(\overset{*}{x}'_G, \overset{*}{x}'_M)$ which represents "the least deviation from two ideal points $\overset{*}{x}_G$ and $\overset{*}{x}_M$"; the technique of "the displaced ideal" (cf. Zeleny [57]) could perhaps be used for this purpose, or some technique for evaluating and comparing (and sometimes transforming) shadow costs may be appropriate.

Re 2.22ii): If $\overset{*}{x}_M$ is represented by (a') we have a combined optimal solution for the GP and MOLP parts of (2.4). If $\overset{*}{x}_M$ is represented by (b'), and (a) and (b') are adjacent points, a compromise (non-optimal) solution is found on the edge of the convex region. A point (x'_G, x'_M), in which the relative losses (determined from the shadow costs) in relation to $(\overset{*}{x}_G, \overset{*}{x}_M)$ are equal, could be such a compromise solution - here we could however have a subjective element of deciding on in which proportion to "give up" on the goals in the GP and MOLP parts, respectively. The analysis could be done in the models introduced above.

Re 2.22iii): If $\overset{*}{x}_M$ is represented by (a'), and (a) and (a') are adjacent to (c), the point (or a set of points if more than two dimensions) of intersection between the two regions would represent the combined solution (if (c) is a set, all the corners of the intersection should be evaluated). The points of a set (c) could be evaluated in the GP and MOLP parts of our model in a fashion similar to that of (ii). If x_M is represented by (b'), which is not adjacent to (c), it is necessary to search through the whole set X_M; this could be done with the linear multiparametric programming technique developed by Yu and Zeleny [51], or the enumeration technique introduced by Isermann [22].

Re 2.22iv): Let $\overset{*}{x}_M$ be represented by either (a') or (b'); this is the case where no combined solution exists and non-dominated solutions in the two regions should be compared and traded off against each other. For that purpose we have a technique suggested by Belenson and Kapur [3] in which an approach for the solution of two-person zero-sum games with mixed strategies is applied to determine efficient solutions; another method that could be applied is the sensitivity analysis based on the duality theorem which was developed by Kornbluth [25]. Finally, it seems possible to apply "the displaced ideal" approach formulated by Zeleny [57], who assumes that the rationale of human choice is to be as close as possible to the perceived ideal. This ideal would in our case be some unrealistic and unattainable point above and between the two regions, and the optimal policy would be one of switching between compromise solutions on the two regions.

Then remains, according to our strategy, to decompose the combined solution - given by either $(\overset{*}{x}_G, \overset{*}{x}_M, \overset{*}{w}_M)$ or $(\overset{*}{x}'_G, \overset{*}{x}'_M, \overset{*}{w}_M)$ - to solutions in MP_1 and MP_2 and determine the requirements both for these solutions to be optimal and for optimal solutions to exist simultaneously in MP_1 - MP_3. The solution vector for the GP part of (2.4) is either $\overset{*}{x}_G$ or $\overset{*}{x}'_G$:

$$\overset{*}{x}_G \ni \overset{*}{x}_{j_1} = \bar{\varepsilon}_{j_1}^{(2)}, \qquad \text{where } j_1 = 1, \ldots, m_1 - 1$$

$$\overset{*}{x}_{m_1} = B_{31} - \sum_{j_1} \bar{\varepsilon}_{j_1}^{(2)} - \sum_{j_2} \bar{\varepsilon}_{j2}^{(1)}$$

$$\overset{*}{x}_{j_2} = \bar{\varepsilon}_{j_2}^{(1)}, \qquad \text{where } j_2 = m_1 + 1, \ldots, n_3$$

or correspondingly:

$$\overset{*}{x}'_G \ni \overset{*}{x}_{j_1} = \bar{\varepsilon}_{j1}^{(4)}, \qquad \text{where } j_1 = 1, \ldots, m_1 - 1$$

$$\overset{*}{x}_{m_1} = B_{31} - \sum_{j_1} \bar{\varepsilon}_{j_1}^{(4)} - \sum_{j_2} \bar{\varepsilon}_{j2}^{(3)}$$

$$\overset{*}{x}_{j_2} = \bar{\varepsilon}_{j_2}^{(3)}, \qquad \text{where } j_2 = m_1 + 1, \ldots, n_3, \tag{2.14'}$$

and $\bar{\varepsilon}^{(3)}$, $\bar{\varepsilon}^{(4)}$ are modifications of $\bar{\varepsilon}^{(1)}$ and $\bar{\varepsilon}^{(2)}$ which are necessary to obtain a combined solution (cf.i)-iv) above). In both cases, however, there will remain deviations (cf. (2.7)) $|\overset{*}{x}_j - g_j| = \overset{*}{\Delta}_j$ about which it is known that for most j, $\overset{*}{\Delta}_j = 0$. As both positive and negative deviations are identified in a GP model, it is also known that if $\overset{*}{\Delta}{}_j^+ > 0$ then $\overset{*}{\Delta}{}_j^- = 0$. We have

$$F^+ = \overset{*}{\Delta}{}_j^+/\gamma_1, \qquad \text{for } j = 1, \ldots, k$$

$$F^- = \overset{*}{\Delta}{}_j^-/\gamma_1$$

$$G^+ = \overset{*}{\Delta}{}_j^+/\gamma_2, \qquad \text{for } j = k + 1, \ldots, n_3$$

$$G^- = \overset{*}{\Delta}{}_j^-/\gamma_2 \tag{2.23}$$

and substitution in (2.2) and (2.3) will give the following (normal) linear-programming models:

$$\begin{aligned} MP'_1 &: \max cy \\ &\quad \text{s.t. } A_1 y = B_1 + F^+ - F^- \\ &\qquad\quad y \geq 0 \\ MP'_2 &: \max dz \\ &\quad \text{s.t. } A_2 z = B_2 + G^+ - G^- \\ &\qquad\quad z \geq 0 \end{aligned} \tag{2.24}$$

in which optimal solutions can be found, if the constraints form a convex region and there exist feasible solutions for non-negative y and z. These are the requirements for MP_1 and MP_2 to have optimal solutions and for optimal solutions to exist simultaneously in MP_1 - MP_3. Then the solution $(\overset{*}{y}, \overset{*}{z}, \overset{*}{x}_G, \overset{*}{x}_M, \overset{*}{w}_M)$, or $(\overset{*}{y}, \overset{*}{z}, \overset{*}{x}'_G, \overset{*}{x}'_M, \overset{*}{w}_M)$, is optimal for our production planning problem; this optimality is, however, in some cases not as abosolute as we may have expected due to the compromise solutions we may have to use for tackling (2.4).

Our final task is to assess to what degree the complexity of the original problem is preserved through the solving process applied in this approach. The decisive simplifications were made when forming mathematical programming models:

- the problem is formulated in one-dimensional time-independent alternative courses of action,
- no other interdependences than those covered by linear functions can be applied,
- there is little flexibility in representing objective structures, as they should be captured in either linear objective functions or linear constraints,
- conflicts among the objectives cannot be tackled as they are represented by infeasible solutions.

These simplifications may be crucial in some problem context, but it could also be the case that the most relevant aspects are covered in a mathematical programming approach. And it is clearly possible to carry out an aggregation/disaggregation process in terms of mathematical programming models: the composite optimal solution obtained in MP_3 was disaggregated to MP_1 and MP_2, and a similar, but contrary, process could be carried out from optimal solutions in MP_1 and MP_2, and would single out a particular corner, an edge or a region in the convex hull forming the GP part of MP_3.

As can be seen from this discussion, we have to go into fairly intricate constructions in order to get a composite optimal solution, i.e. in order to evaluate and assess interdependent objectives against a higher level (strategic) plan. Then, how well did we succeed in relation to the obstacles described in the case text? We have the following results (cf section 1.3):

. Re (1.1) the MOLP-approach shows how to create a tactical plan for attaining n_i objectives - if the MOLP-formulation is an appropriate representation of the problem at hand;

. Re (1.2) the principle of a composite optimal solution shows how to evaluate and assess (or adapt) objectives in the light of a higher level (strategic) plan, here represented by $A_3^{(h+1)}$;

. Re (1.3) the composition/decomposition scheme between MP_3 and MP_1 - MP_2 is a scheme for assessing the relevance and relative importance of the objectives of $A_1^{(h)}$ and $A_2^{(h)}$, i.e. divisional objectives, for example;

. Re (1.4) only simple forms for supporting interdependences among the objectives can be handled through objective functions and constraints; conflicts will result in infeasibilities;

. Re (1.5) this obstacle cannot be handled;

Then we may conclude that the MOLP-approach represents a fairly complex, and mathematically involved way of conceptualizing the MCDM-area. It belongs to the decision analysis - operations (or adaptation) objectives - analytical way of working in a management context. It has some drawbacks (cf our four steps of conceptual delimitation in section 1): (i) the set of alternative courses of action is not extendable; (ii) all decision-making activities should be covered by a mathematical programming formulation; (iii) problems involving multiple criteria can be solved only if the assumptions necessary for the MOLP-model are not too restrictive; (iv) the MOLP-model belongs to levels (ii) and (iii) of description, and is not very useful for problem-solving as there are very few commercial MOLP-packages available.

Let us then move on to another approach - the fuzzy MOLP-approach.

3. FUZZY MULTIPLE OBJECTIVE LINEAR PROGRAMMING

The fuzzy multiple-objective linear-programming (or F-MOLP) approach is a level (ii) modelling approach, which may be extended to both level (i) and level (iii) modelling, as the approach is made fairly flexible by the elements of fuzziness introduced. In Johnsen's scheme it may be classified with the "cube" for decision analysis - operations objectives - analytic means; there are, however, alternatives to both operations objectives - adaptation/development objectives - and to analytic means - the fuzzy set representations require interactive means. Then the first impression is that the F-MOLP is more flexible than the MOLP-approach. Some work has been done on F-MOLP (cf [19],[35],[46] , [47]) but here we shall mainly draw upon some previous work (cf [12],[13]).

As in the previous section we shall try to pinpoint one control aspect of the problem situation described in the case text in section 1.3: the <u>interdependence</u> of objectives, and find out how that can be tackled with the help of the theory of fuzzysets. As in the previous section, we will not work with all the objectives G_1 - G_8, but limit ourselves to four; the results are easily extended to any number or objectives.

For our present purposes it will be enough to consider a situation with four objectives (cf. Fig. 4). The structure shown in Fig. 4 is only one of several possible structures with four objectives, but it shows the three different kinds of interdependent objectives we will deal with in this context.

(i) conflict (G_1 and G_2),
(ii) mutual support (G_2 and G_3, G_3 and G_4),
(iii) unilateral support (G_3 and G_1, G_2 and G_4). (3.1)

If the concept of optimality can be regarded as trivial in a single objective situation, it is almost as trivial to state that the objectives in a situation of multiple objectives can be expected to be interdependent.

The four objectives will all be taken to be fuzzy sets in A, the given set of alternative courses of action (as in [1]):

$$G_j = \{(a_i, \mu_{G_j}(a_i)\} , \quad \forall i \in [1, n], \text{ where } a_i \in A \text{ and } \mu_{G_j} : A \rightarrow [0, 1], \quad j = [1, 4]. \qquad (3.2)$$

Let us find out if we can deal with the three forms of interdependence in this context: the membership functions μ_{G_j} represent a decision-maker's evaluation of to what extent the alternatives a_i produce an attainment of each one of the objectives G_j.

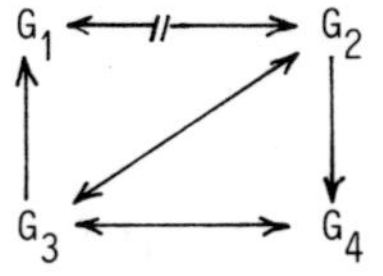

Fig. 4 A structure of four interdependent objectives.

Interdependence means that the cases in which an objective is attained cannot occur independently, but that an alternative a_i which is "satisfactory" for G_1 (for instance) is "not satisfactory" for G_2, and was found "satisfactory" for G_1 because it was "rather satisfactory" for G_3 (cf. Fig. 1). The decision problem in such a case is to find some alternative a* which both resolves the conflict (G_1 - G_2) and is the one found "most satisfactory". Such an alternative does not exist in a non-fuzzy formulation - the conflict is a guarantee of that - but the imprecision of a fuzzy formulation should offer us ways of finding, or even creating an operational alternative.

Let us consider A as a universe and let f be an ordinary function from A to another universe B: $a \in A \rightarrow f(a) \in B$. Now it can be shown (cf. [19], where several methods are given) that f could be defined for a fuzzy domain - and given a fuzzy range as well - iff,

$$\mu_{H_j}(f(a_i)) \geq \mu_{G_j}(a_i), \quad \forall a_i \in A, \; i \in [1, n] \tag{3.3}$$

where G_j is a fuzzy subset of A, and H_j a corresponding fuzzy subset of B; the universe B is introduced as a simplification - interdependence could be discussed in A, or the mapping through f could be onto A - and for simplicity we have postponed declaring the dimensionality of A and B. The aim of the function f (which would be a class of n functions, if A and B are defined in n-dimensional spaces) is to transform cases of interdependence to a space in which evaluation and comparison of the objectives is possible.

<u>Conflicting objectives</u>: an alternative a_i, for which $\mu_{G_1}(a_i) \approx 0$, will have $\mu_{G_2}(a_i) \approx 1$; then for an appropriate function f it should be possible to find a $f(a_i)$ for which $\mu_{H_1}(f(a_i))$ is "not too close to 0", and $\mu_{H_2}(f(a_i))$ is "not too close to 1", i.e. a point of compromise like "rather low on H_1 and rather high on H_2":

$$(\mu_{H_1} \wedge \mu_{H_2})(f(a_i)).$$

<u>Mutually supportive objectives</u>: an alternative a_i, for which $\mu_{G_2}(a_i)$ is "rather close to 1", will have $\mu_{G_3}(a_i)$ "closer to 1"; an alternative a_j, for which $\mu_{G_3}(a_j)$ is "rather close to 1", will have $\mu_{G_2}(a_j)$ "closer to 1"; with an appropriate f we should find a $f(a_j)$ for which $\mu_{H_2}(f(a_i))$ is "rather close to 1" and $\mu_{H_3}(f(a\ ))$ is "closer to 1", and vice versa, so that $f(a_k) = \max_{i,j}(\mu_{H_2} \wedge \mu_{H_3})(f(a_i), f(a_j))$, i.e. there is an alternative $a_k (i,j,k \in [1, n])$ such that both $\mu_{H_2}(f(a_k)$ and $\mu_{H_3}(f(a_k))$ are at least "almost 1".

<u>Unilaterally supportive objectives</u>; an alternative a_i, for which $\mu_{G_2}(a_i)$ is "rather close to 1" will result in $\mu_{G_4}(a_i)$ being "closer to 1"; for an appropriate function f there should then be a $f(a_i)$ for which $\mu_{H_2}(f(a_i))$ is at least "rather close to 1" so that $\mu_{H_4}(f(a_i))$ will be "closer to 1".

These three cases can be illustrated as in Fig. 5

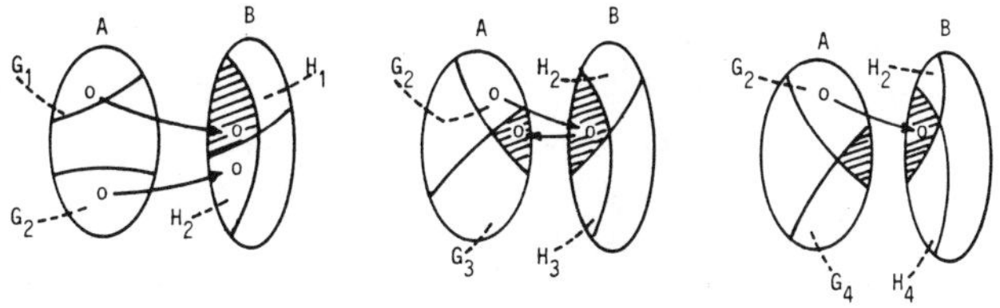

Fig. 5. An illustration of interdependent objectives.

In order to represent the multigoal situation shown in fig. 4 the three illustrations should be superimposed on each other, which - with an appropriate arrangement of the goal sets - will give Fig. 6 (the o's indicate some points).

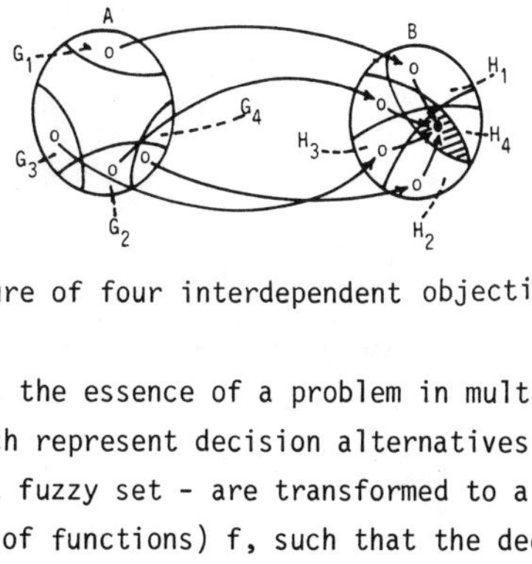

Fig. 6. A structure of four interdependent objectives.

Fig. 6 then shows the essence of a problem in multiple objectives: points in the universe A - which represent decision alternatives satisfying at least one objective defined as a fuzzy set - are transformed to a universe B by means of a function (or a class of functions) f, such that the decision alternatives may be evaluated against more than one objective, after which we shall just have to find an alternative (• in Fig. 6) which in some systematic way can be shown to be "most satisfactory" for all the objectives when their interdependence is either accounted for and/or used.

The "most satisfactory" alternative is found as (cf.[4]),

$$a^* = \max \left[\mu_{H_1}(f(a_i)) \wedge \mu_{H_2}(f(a_i)) \wedge \mu_{H_3}(f(a_i)) \wedge \mu_{H_4}(f(a_i))\right], \forall a_i \in A, \qquad (3.4)$$

which only outlines the principle: the difficult part is to formulate an algorithm which both deals with the interdependence and finds either a "best" alternative or a subset of "satisfactory" alternatives. The min-operator used by Bellman-Zadeh does not account for the interdependence, and gives rather a poor performance for conflicting objectives; what is needed is some construction along the following lines:

According to (3.3) $\mu_{H_j}(f(a_i)) \geq \mu_{G_j}(a_i)$, $\forall a_i \in A$, and as decision alternatives are evaluated in B it is possible to establish ranking relations among them relative to each one of H_1 - H_4 (= the corresponding membership values); let the corresponding fuzzy subsets be A_1 - A_4. Then we have for every subset A_j, starting with the element $a_i^{(j)}$ of the highest rank,

$$\mu_k^{(j)}(a_i) : a_i^{(j)} \rightarrow [0, 1], \forall k \in [1, 4] \text{ but } j \neq k \qquad (3.5)$$

which is a subjective assessment of how satisfactory the alternative is in relation to each one of the k objectives other than j, taking into account their interdependence with the objective j. The membership values in (3.5) are developed $\forall i$ and $\forall j$, and the resulting values will then be systematic - but subjective - evaluations of all the decision alternatives against all the objectives. The next step is to find a consistent method for assessing to what degree the decision alternatives outperform each other in terms of overall attainment of the objectives; this could, for example, be done as follows:

(i) consider an $a_i^{(j)}$,

(ii) compute $\alpha_i^{(j)} = 1 - (\bigwedge \mu_k^{(j)}(a\ )), \quad k \in [1, 4]$, but $j \neq k$ (3.6)

(iii) use $\mu_j^{\alpha_i}(f(a_i))$ as an assessment of how satisfactory the alternative a_i is.

Here (3.6) (ii) can be computed with the min-operator; then (3.4) can be modified to

$$a^* = \max[\bigwedge \mu_{H_j}^{\alpha_i(j)}] \ , \quad \forall a_i \in A \text{ and } \forall j \in [1, 4], \qquad (3.4')$$

and the min-operator - although with some misgivings - may be used. This procedure is illustrated with a simple numerical example, see Fig. 7 (7 alternatives, 4 goals with the structure shown in Fig. 4); (3.5) is shown in M_1 - M_4; (3.6) (ii) in $\hat{M}$; (3.6) (iii) in M*). According to (3.4') $a^* = a_4$, and the ranking of the alternatives is given by $[a_4, a_7, a_6, a_3, a_5, a_2, a_1]$.

This simple example demonstrates two things:

(i) a simple and intuitively acceptable modification of the Bellman-Zadeh approach gives an answer also in the case of interdependent objectives, but

(ii) this approach is completely dependent upon the subjective evaluation done by the decision-maker.

Thus the example also demonstrates the need for an algorithm to realize the described approach in a systematic - and formally acceptable - way. There seem to be three prerequisites for that:

(i) an <u>alternative</u> for the min-operator, which appears too restrictive (cf.[19]);

(ii) a systematic method for <u>evaluating</u> the effects of interdependent objectives on the process of comparing alternatives (cf. the method of the displaced ideal in [58]);

(iii) an efficient <u>interactive</u> method for creating the necessary membership functions.

M_1

$a_i^{(1)}$	G_2	G_3	G_4
0.85	0.15	0.60	0.10
0.75	0.25	0.50	0.70
0.65	0.35	0.45	0.30
0.90	0.10	0.20	0.45
0.80	0.20	0.25	0.60
0.95	0.05	0.30	0.50
0.65	0.35	0.70	0.25

M_2

$a_i^{(2)}$	G_1	G_3	G_4
0.65	0.35	0.70	0.80
0.75	0.25	0.80	0.85
0.85	0.15	0.85	0.90
0.60	0.40	0.65	0.85
0.70	0.30	0.75	0.75
0.55	0.45	0.60	0.65
0.85	0.15	0.90	0.90

M_3

$a_i^{(3)}$	G_1	G_2	G_4
0.55	0.70	0.75	0.60
0.40	0.60	0.50	0.50
0.60	0.75	0.85	0.65
0.50	0.65	0.60	0.70
0.50	0.70	0.75	0.55
0.55	0.70	0.60	0.60
0.60	0.75	0.80	0.70

M_4

$a_i^{(4)}$	G_1	G_2	G_3
0.60	0.10	0.40	0.70
0.50	0.70	0.35	0.60
0.60	0.30	0.40	0.75
0.65	0.45	0.35	0.80
0.50	0.60	0.30	0.70
0.60	0.50	0.25	0.75
0.75	0.25	0.45	0.85

$\hat{M}$

a_i	$\alpha_i^{(1)}$	$\alpha_i^{(2)}$	$\alpha_i^{(3)}$	$\alpha_i^{(4)}$
a_1	0.90	0.65	0.40	0.90
a_2	0.75	0.75	0.50	0.65
a_3	0.70	0.85	0.35	0.70
a_4	0.90	0.60	0.40	0.65
a_5	0.80	0.70	0.45	0.70
a_6	0.95	0.55	0.40	0.75
a_7	0.75	0.85	0.30	0.75

M^*

a_1	G_1	G_2	G_3	G_4	Min
a_1	0.864	0.756	0.787	0.631	0.631
a_2	0.806	0.806	0.632	0.637	0.632
a_3	0.740	0.871	0.836	0.699	0.699
a_4	0.909	0.736	0.758	0.756	0.736
a_5	0.837	0.779	0.671	0.837	0.671
a_6	0.952	0.720	0.787	0.841	0.720
a_7	0.724	0.871	0.858	0.806	0.724

Fig. 7. A test of a fuzzy method for assessing interdependent objectives.

Some work has been done on these prerequisites (cf. [4,18,19,27,31,35,38,39,49,55,56] but there is still no generally accepted method available which could deal with all the prerequisities.

Another point to be made is that both objectives and decision alternatives should be described in terms of multiple attributes (cf [22]), and not in the simplified form described here. This adds to the complexity of a decision problem in multiple interacting objectives as the forms for interaction may vary, and should be evaluated across the attributes. Besides the problems with inconsistencies such evaluations involve several scale transformations and related decisions regarding comparable dimensions.

Let us turn to a special case in which some of the problems mentioned can be solved: a multiple objective problem formulated with the help of a fuzzy mathematical programming framework. There are several contributions to the fuzzy MP-model (cf,[4, 31, 35, 46, 47, 56, 58, 59]), but here we will develop a model for fuzzy multiobjective programming based on some results by Takeda and Nishida [44] and some previous work (cf [13]):

Let us describe the set A of alternative courses of action with the elements of a decision space X defined by,

$$X = \{ x \in \mathbb{R}^n \mid f(x) \geq 0 \} \tag{3.7}$$

where $f(x) = (f_1(x), f_2(x), \ldots, f_m(x))$ are m criteria functions. Takeda and Nishida [44] showed that a fuzzy set $N[X \mid \Lambda]$ of non-dominated solutions in a multiple criteria problem, with a fuzzy domination structure Λ can be approximated with a fuzzy set $O\ [X \mid \Lambda^*]$ of solutions, which represents the maximum of the weighted sum of the criteria functions with weights derived from a fuzzy polar cone. What is then the relevance of this result?

Consider $X \sqsubset \mathbb{R}^n$ and a criteria space $Y = h[X]$, where $y \sqsubset \mathbb{R}^1$; for any point $y \in Y$, let $D(y)$ be a fuzzy set in $\mathbb{R}^1$, with membership function $\mu_{D(y)}$, such that $\mu_{D(y)}(d)$, where $d = g(y', y)$, is the grade of membership for y' to be dominated by y ($\mu_{D(y)}(0) = 1$ for all $y \in Y$). The family $\{D(y) \mid y \in Y\}$ is called the <u>fuzzy domination structure</u> in Y; it is convenient to decompose D(y) into its constituent level sets and to assume, without much loss of generality, that D(y) is a fuzzy convex cone Λ.

This is possible if $\sup \mu_{D(y)}(d)$, for $y \in Y$ and $y' = y$, is taken to be the degree for y' to be dominated, and thus $\mu_N(y') = 1 - \sup \mu_{D(y)}(d)$ to be the membership function defining the set N of all non-dominated solutions in Y.

Then it is easy to define level sets as $\Lambda_\alpha = \{ d \in \mathbb{R}^1 \mid \mu_\Lambda(d) \geq \alpha \}$, where the levels α may be chosen subjectively, and the structure is given by the grade of membership of dominance. If Λ_α, $\forall \alpha$, are convex cones, the fuzzy set Λ is also a convex cone; a fuzzy set Λ in $\mathbb{R}^1$ is a convex cone iff $\mu_\Lambda(d) = \mu_\Lambda(\gamma \cdot d), \gamma > 0$, $\forall d \neq 0$, $d \in \mathbb{R}^1$ and $\mu_\Lambda(d) = 1$ for $d = 0$.

In this way we get the fuzzy set $N[X \mid \Lambda]$ of non-dominated solutions, with a fuzzy domination structure in the form of a fuzzy convex cone (as $X = h^{-1}(Y)$).

Compared with (3.5) - (3.6) the fuzzy set of non-dominated solutions is of a higher level of abstraction:

(i) the alternatives are explicitly multidimensional and described numerically;
(ii) the assessment of the grade of dominance of one alternative over another is made in an overall fashion for all the objectives;
(iii) interactions among the objectives are not assessed explicitly, but $N[X \mid \ ]$ can serve as a basis for an operational and efficient algorithm.

The set $N[X \mid \ ]$ is important as it gives us both the non-dominated solutions, and a fuzzy domination structure for the dominated solutions. The non-dominated solutions may, however, be numerous, and we should find a way to select a "best" solution among them. This is where the approximation $O[X \mid \Lambda^*]$ is useful (cf.[12] for details).

Let us return to the criteria space Y: Takeda and Nishida [44] show that $N[Y \mid \Lambda]$ can be "squeezed" between two approximations,

$$O[Y \mid \Lambda^+] \sqsubset N[Y \mid \Lambda] \sqsubset O[Y \mid \Lambda^*] \tag{3.8}$$

the inner and outer approximate fuzzy sets, respectively, Λ^* is a fuzzy polar cone: given a fuzzy convex cone Λ, its fuzzy polar cone Λ^* is defined as $\Lambda^* = \bigsqcup_{0 \leq \alpha \leq 1} \alpha \Lambda^*_{1-\alpha}$. Takeda and Nishida show that Λ^* is a convex cone and that its membership function μ_{Λ^*} is quasi-concave and upper semicontinuous on S, which is a simplex in $\mathbb{R}^1$. The cone Λ^* may be interpreted as a fuzzy set of optimum weighting factors, and $O[Y \mid \Lambda^*]$ as a fuzzy set of solutions in Y which is the maximum of the weighted sum of the criteria; the problem of finding $O[Y \mid \Lambda^*]$ is thus an ordinary mathematical programming problem.

Let us then define a fuzzy set Λ^+ for a given Λ by $\Lambda^+ = \bigsqcup \alpha \text{ Int } \lambda^*_{1-\alpha}$ for which it can be shown (cf. [44]) that for the fuzzy set $0 [Y \mid \text{Int } \Lambda^*_\alpha] = \{ Y^0(\lambda) \mid \lambda \in \text{Int } \Lambda^*_\alpha \}$, as for any fuzzy polar cone Λ^* : $0 [Y \mid \Lambda^*] = \bigsqcup_{0<\alpha<1} \alpha 0 [Y \mid \Lambda^*_{1-\alpha}]$, and for a given fuzzy domination structure Λ, $0 [Y \mid \Lambda^+] = \bigsqcup \alpha \; 0 [Y \mid \text{Int } \Lambda^*_{1-\alpha}]$, as it was shown by Yu [51] that for an ordinary domination structure Λ, $\{ Y^0(\lambda) \; \lambda \in \text{Int } \Lambda^* \} \sqsubset N [Y \mid \Lambda]$; here $Y^0(\lambda) = \{ y^0 \in Y \mid \lambda \cdot y^0 = \max \lambda \cdot y, y \in Y \}$. Then it can be proved (cf [44]) that $0 [Y \mid \Lambda^+] \sqsubset N [Y \mid \Lambda]$, and we get the inner approximation of $N [Y \mid \Lambda]$.

For the next step we would need some means for transforming the fuzzy domination structure from the criteria space to the decision space in order to guide the selection of decision alternatives. This involves solving a vector maximization problem with multiple criteria and with a fuzzy domination structure: such means are not yet available. Consequently, we shall have to resort to an approximation, which can be found from the fuzzy mathematical programming technique.

Consider the following multiobjective programming problem:

$$
\begin{aligned}
\max \; & [C(X) \mid \Lambda] \\
& = \max [c_1,(x), c_2(x), \ldots, c_m(x)], \\
\text{s.t.} \; & Ax \simeq b, \\
& x \geq 0, \\
& x \in X
\end{aligned}
\tag{3.9}
$$

where ($\simeq$) denotes a fuzzy constraint, i.e. we have membership functions,

$$
\mu_{b_i} = \begin{cases} 1 & \text{if } (Ax)_i \leq b_i, \\ 1 - \dfrac{(Ax)_i - b_i}{\delta_i} & \text{if } b_i < (Ax)_i \leq b_i + \delta_i, \\ 0 & \text{if } (Ax)_i > b_i + \delta_i \end{cases}
\tag{3.10}
$$

which indicate that there are degrees of allowable violations of the constraints; $(Ax)_i$ refers to the ith row of the matrix of constraints. Let μ_b denote the combination $\mu_b = \mu_{b_1} \wedge \mu_{b_2} \wedge \ldots \wedge \mu_{b_i} \wedge \ldots \wedge \mu_{b_k}$ of these membership functions; this combination is normally carried out with the min-operator (cf. [4,46,48,52]) and represents the fuzzy set of feasible alternatives. Now we have three possible combinations:

(i) $\mu_{[C(X) \mid \Lambda^*]} \wedge \mu_b$: a fuzzy Pareto-optimal decision,

(ii) $\mu_{[C(X)|\ \Lambda^+]} \wedge \mu_b$: a fuzzy decision based on optimal trade-offs

(iii) $\mu_{[N(X)|\ \Lambda]} \wedge \mu_b$: a set of feasible, non-dominated fuzzy decisions (3.11)

where $\mu_{[C(X)|\ \Lambda^*]}$, $\mu_{[C(X)|\ \Lambda^+]}$ and $\mu_{[N(X)|\ \Lambda]}$ will have to be formulated as fuzzy constraints which are subjective, intuitive, scalar-valued representations of the true cone dominance structures Λ^*, Λ^+ and Λ. Of these sets of membership functions $\mu_{[N(X)|\Lambda]}$ is the set most difficult to grasp intuitively and to give an appropriate formulation.

There are some methods available with features approaching those described as desirable: compromise programming, introduced by Zeleny [56], in which the non-dominated solutions are evaluated in relation to some chosen or constructed ideal point; introducing ordinal preferences for non-dominated solutions - as suggested by Yager [47],[48] - conveys a decision-maker's own assessment of the relative importance of the goals; Takeda and Nishida [44] assumed that the criteria functions are concave and continuously differentiable over X, and applied the Kuhn-Tucker theorem; in Carlsson [12] a simple measure of "relative closeness", based explicitly on the interdependence of the goals, was suggested; Zeleny's [57] theory of the displaced ideal would, it seems, also be very useful in a fuzzy adaptation.

Besides these approaches there is also the possibility of using a trial and error method through parametric programming and successive modifications of the constraints. For that purpose any standard LP-package may be applied; it is a known and proved result (cf. [46], and also [11,15,19,47,48] that (3.9) - (3.10) may be rewritten in the following form:

$$\begin{aligned} &\max \quad \lambda \\ &\text{s.t.} \quad \lambda\, \delta_i + (A'x)_i \leq b'_i + \delta_i, \\ &\qquad\quad x \geq 0 \end{aligned} \tag{3.12}$$

where i denotes the ith row of the system of equations; A' is the matrix A combined with the criteria functions C(X). This is a standard LP-form.

The F-MOLP approach seems to be no less complex than the MOLP-model, even if it is more flexible due to the introduction of fuzzy set-based techniques; the reliance on the decision-maker to provide membership functions is both a positive and a negative feature of the technique: positive, because the decision-maker's experience and intuition may be put to service; negative, because subjective assessments could be badly misleading. Let us then find out to what extent the method is able to overcome the obstacles described in the case text:

. Re (1.1) the F-MOLP approach is a true multi-objective method, and shows how n_i objectives could be attained; the F-MOLP is more flexible than the MOLP-method because of the subjective membership functions, which can be given any appropriate form;

. Re (1.2) the evaluation of objectives in the light of a higher level (strategic) plan is not dealt with; the F-MOLP could obviously be used in the same fashion as the MOLP-approach of the previous section;

. Re (1.3) the relevance and relative importance of the objectives are assessed through the fuzzy domination structure, which - in principle - serves as the desired scheme;

. Re (1.4) the F-MOLP approach was developed primarily for handling interdependent objectives; as is shown, fuzzy set theory offers means for that purpose;

. Re (1.5) degrees of attainment for the objectives can be represented with the help of membership functions, and comparison with and evaluation against different options for an overall policy are handled through the fuzzy domination structure;

Then we may conclude that the F-MOLP approach is a mathematically rather involved and complex conceptualization of the MCDM-area, although the use of fuzzy sets is a promising innovation. The approach was described as belonging to the decision analysis - operations/adaptation/development objectives - analytical/interactive way of working in a management context; the many alternatives are due to the effects of the use of subjective membership functions. There are some limitations with the F-MOLP (cf the four steps of conceptual delimitation in section 1): (i) the set of alternative courses of action is given initially, but can be modified (but not extended) through the membership functions; (ii) all decision-making activities should be covered by the F-MOLP model; (iii) problems in multiple criteria can be solved to the extent that the assumptions forming the basis of the method do not make solutions irrelevant; (iv) F-MOLP is mainly a level (ii) method, but could be used both on levels (i) and (iii); no commercial packages are available, although some successful experiments have been made with the IFPS/Optimum package (cf [13]) thus, F-MOLP is not yet very useful for real life problem-solving.

Let us then move on to quite a different way of conceptualizing the MCDM-area - a systems approach.

4. A SYSTEMS APPROACH TO MCDM

Ackoff [1] argues that science-oriented methodology, which he characterizes as (i) analysis-oriented, (ii) reductionistic and (iii) mechanistic, is not appropriate for tackling management problems, as (cf [1] , pp 237-239):

"... what decision makers deal with, I maintain, are messes, not problems ..."

and a "mess" is described as a system of external conditions that produces dissatisfaction;

"The 'solution' to a 'mess' - whatever it may be - is not the simple sum of the solutions of the problems which are or can be extracted from it. No 'mess' can be solved by solving each of its component problems independently of the others, because no mess can be decomposed into independent problems..."

This leads to the argument that a methodology for tackling decision problems should be (i) synthesis-oriented and (ii) expansionistic. And furthermore,

"Because many problems do not remain solved and because many that can be solved change in significant ways while being solved, to pursue their solutions - optimal, satisficing, or any other brand - is to pursue a mirage ... Problem solving is not only a means to an end; to many it is also an end-in-itself."

This indicates that the problem-solving tools should emphasize (iii) adaptation and learning, instead of being algorithms which operate in terms of simple, mechanistic cause-effect relationships. This point (iii) implies that the decision-maker should be directly involved in the problem-solving process.

Here we will try out Ackoff's recommendation as a means for conceptualizing the MCDM-area. As the theory of fuzzy sets appears rather promising - even to some extent fascinating - we will study a systems approach which is based on fuzzy systems elements (for details cf [9]).

Let us consider a decision-maker DM for an interval $[t_1, t_n]$ and assume that there is available to him a family $\mathbf{A}$ of alternative courses of action in that interval (we have immediately extended A_1 - A_5 to the family A):

$$\mathbf{A}_{[t_1,\, t_n]} = \{\mathbf{A}_1, \mathbf{A}_2, \ldots, \mathbf{A}_n\} \qquad (4.1)$$

so that a set $\mathbf{A}_i$ is associated with each point of time t_i. We will, furthermore, assume that each set $\mathbf{A}_i$ (for $[t_1, t_n]$ consists of k activities described by k attribute sets:

$$\mathbf{A}_i = \{ A_{i1}, A_{i2}, \ldots, A_{ik} \}, \quad k = k(i), \tag{4.2}$$

and that each attribute set A_{ik} is an m-dimensional , numerical description of an action k in Euclidean space,

$$A_{ik} \sqsubseteq \mathbf{R}^m \tag{4.3}$$

Thus the attribute set A_{ik} is finite,

$$A_{ik} \ni \{ a_{k1}, a_{k2}, \ldots, a_{km} \} \tag{4.4}$$

and DM is expected to have access to these elements (in some convenient way). Let there also be a family of external events,

$$\mathbf{E}_{[t_1, t_n]} = \{ \mathbf{E}_1, \mathbf{E}_2, \ldots, \mathbf{E}_v \} \tag{4.5}$$

which DM cannot influence, but which he perceives and is able to describe in some way: each set $\mathbf{E}_j$ is thus associated with a t_j, consists of k events and is described by k attribute sets,

$$\mathbf{E}_j = \{ E_{j1}, E_{j2}, \ldots, E_{jk} \}, \; k = k(j), \tag{4.6}$$

such that each attribute set, analogously, is an m-dimensional, numerical description of an external activity k in Euclidean space,

$$E_{jk} \sqsubseteq \mathbf{R}^m \tag{4.7}$$

so that the set E_{jk} is finite,

$$E_{jk} \ni \{ e_{k1}, e_{k2}, \ldots, e_{km} \} \tag{4.8}$$

Consider then the fuzzy sets X_{ik}, Y_{jk} which are defined by,

$$X_{ik} = \{ a_{km}, \mu_X(a_{km}) \}, \; \forall m, \text{ where } a_{km} \in A_{ik},$$

$$Y_{jk} = \{ e_{km}, \; \gamma(e_{km}) \}, \; \forall m, \text{ where } e_{km} \in E_{jk}, \tag{4.9}$$

$$\mu_X(a_{km}) : A_{ik} \rightarrow [0, 1] , \text{ if } \forall m$$
$$\mu_Y(e_{km}) : E_{jk} \rightarrow [0, 1] , \text{ if } \forall m \quad (4.10)$$

$$\mathbf{X}_i = \{ X_{i1}, X_{i2}, \ldots, X_{ik} \}$$
$$\mathbf{Y}_j = \{ Y_{j1}, Y_{j2}, \ldots, Y_{jk} \} \quad (4.11)$$

$$\mathbf{X}_{[t_1, t_n]} = \{ \mathbf{X}_1, \mathbf{X}_2, \ldots, \mathbf{X}_n \}$$
$$\mathbf{Y}_{[t_1, t_n]} = \{ \mathbf{Y}_1, \mathbf{Y}_2, \ldots, \mathbf{Y}_v \} \quad (4.12)$$

and are given a structure which corresponds to that of **A** and **E**. Now, however, DM is not requested to give crisp, numerical assessments of the attributes, but is allowed to use imprecision, and assessments in degrees, when formulating the membership functions μ_X and μ_Y. Fuzzy attribute descriptions allow a closer reproduction of the "true flavour" of actions and external events.

The fuzzy sets of (4.9) - (4.12) are time-dependent, Euclidean mappings; Lientz' [28] formulation of time-dependent fuzzy sets is analogous, if considered at discrete points of time.

As DM was expected to provide the information which is necessary for formulating (4.1) - (4.8), we will also assume that he is able to give us the necessary membership functions for (4.9) - (4.12). We will, furthermore, assume that each set A_i is organized hierarchically in order to make it easier for DM to handle: let H be a finite, partially ordered set $\sqsubseteq \mathbf{R}^1$, i.e. there is a binary relation R(h,H), such that

$$(h_1, h_2) \; \varepsilon \; R \text{ for all } h \; \varepsilon \; H$$
$$(h_1, h_2) \; \varepsilon \; R \text{ and } h_1 \neq h_2, \text{ then } (h_2, h_1) \not\varepsilon R$$
$$(h_1, h_2) \; \varepsilon \; R \text{ and } (h_2, h_3) \; \varepsilon \; R, \text{ then } (h_1, h_3) \; \varepsilon \; R \quad (4.13)$$

This relation may be denoted by $\lesssim$. When applied to $\mathbf{A}_{[t_1, t_n]}$ it will introduce a hierarchical structure in both the family and its constituent sets: let h = 0, 1, ..., h*-1, h* be ordered according to R(h, H), and consider $\mathbf{A}_i$ defined by (4.2) - (4.4):

$$\overset{*}{\mathbf{A}}{}_i^{(h)} \sqsupseteq \{ (\overset{*}{A}{}_{i1}^{(h)} , \overset{*}{A}{}_{i2}^{(h)} , \ldots, \overset{*}{A}{}_{iq}^{(h)} , \; (\overset{*}{A}{}_{i1}^{(h-1)} , \overset{*}{A}{}_{i2}^{(h-1)} , \ldots, \overset{*}{A}{}_{iq}^{(h-1)}) \ldots (A_{i1}^{(1)} ,$$

$A_{i2}^{(1)}, \ldots, A_{iq}^{(1)}), (A_{i1}^{(0)}, A_{i2}^{(0)}, \ldots, A_{iq}^{(0)})\}$, where $1, 2, \ldots, q \in Q_i(h)$, but

$$\sum_{h=1}^{\overset{*}{h}} q(h) = k, \tag{4.14}$$

which is now an hierarchically organized set of actions, described by their correspondingly organized attribute sets. If every $\mathbf{A}_i$ is formulated in this fashion, DM will see his set of actions every t_i as an organized structure in which an action either (i) "supports", (ii) "is supported by", or (iii) "is in parallel to" other actions. These properties are clearly more properly treated if they are regarded as fuzzy - there are normally several degrees of "support". In other words, we should have a fuzzy hierarchical structure in addition to the fuzzy attribute descriptions we have in (4.9) - (4.12); this is achieved if we introduce a fuzzy hierarchical structure in $\mathbf{X}_i$:

$$\mathbf{X}_i \supseteq \{(X_{i1}^{(\overset{*}{h})}, X_{i2}^{(\overset{*}{h})}, \ldots, X_{iq}^{(\overset{*}{h})}), (X_{i1}^{(\overset{*}{h}-1)}, X_{i2}^{(\overset{*}{h}-1)}, \ldots, X_{iq}^{(\overset{*}{h}-1)}) \ldots (X_{i1}^{(1)}, X_{i2}^{(1)}, \ldots, X_{iq}^{(1)}), (X_{i1}^{(0)}, X_{i2}^{(0)}, \ldots, X_{iq}^{(0)})\}, \text{ where } 1, 2, \ldots, q \in Q_i(h),$$

$$\text{but } \sum_{h=1}^{\overset{*}{h}} q(h) = k \tag{4.15}$$

and,

$$X_{iq} = \{ a_{km}, \mu_X(a_{km}), \mu_h(a_{km})\}, \forall m,$$

$$\mu_h(a_{km}) : h \rightarrow [0, 1] , \forall m \tag{4.16}$$

If it is possible to find some relationship between hierarchical levels and attribute descriptions - as some kind of conceptual aggregation - it may be possible to combine the two membership functions,

$$\mu_{X(h)} (a_{km}) = \mu_X(a_{km}) \wedge \mu_h(a_{km}) \tag{4.17}$$

if some appropriate operator could be formulated. Then $\mathbf{X}_i$ would be a fuzzy description of actions - with a fuzzy hierarchical structure - in which the attribute descriptions are dependent upon the hierarchical level of the actions.

The set $\mathbf{Y}_j$ can be given a similar structure, as DM may be expected to organize his observations of external events in a way which is analogous to the structure of his actions:

$$\mathbf{Y}_j \sqsupseteq \{ (Y_{j1}^{(\overset{*}{h})}, Y_{j2}^{(\overset{*}{h})}, \ldots, Y_{jq}^{(\overset{*}{h})}), (Y_{j1}^{(\overset{*}{h}-1)}, \ldots, Y_{jq}^{(\overset{*}{h}-1)}), \ldots,$$

$$(Y_{j1}^{(1)}, Y_{j2}^{(1)}, \ldots, Y_{jq}^{(1)}), (Y_{j1}^{(0)}, Y_{j2}^{(0)}, \ldots, Y_{jq}^{(0)})\}, \text{ where } 1, 2, \ldots, q \varepsilon\, Q_j(h)$$

$$(4.18)$$

$$Y_{jq}^{(h)} = \{ e_{km}, \mu_Y(e_{km}), \mu_h(e_{km}) \}, \forall m,$$

$$\mu_h(e_{km}) : h \rightarrow [0, 1] , \forall m, \text{ or}$$

$$\mu_y(h)(e_{km}) = \mu_Y(e_{km}) \wedge \mu_h(e_{km}) \qquad (4.19)$$

Then we would, finally, have the two families $\mathbf{X} = \{ \mathbf{X}_i, \forall i \}$ and $\mathbf{Y} = \{ \mathbf{Y}_j, \forall_j \}$, which describe actions and external events for an interval $[t_1, t_n]$, so that the descriptions are "relevant" to DM, and organized in a "structurally relevant" way.

Let us then return to the observation that actions "support" each other in varying degrees. We will distinguish between two kinds of supporting relations between two fuzzy actions $X_{ig}^{(h_1)}$ and $X_{ik}^{(h_2)}$ $(g = g(i, h_1), k = k(i, h_2))$

i. $X_{ig}^{(h_1)}$ supports / is supported by $X_{ik}^{(h_2)}$ if $h_1 \neq h_2$

ii. $X_{ig}^{(h_1)}$ is simultaneous with $X_{ik}^{(h_2)}$ if $h_1 = h_2$ (4.20)

As we should allow degrees in the support, let us introduce the following relations:

$$DC((X^{(h_1)} \longrightarrow X^{(h_2)}), \mu_C) \sqsubseteq (X^{(h_1)}, X^{(h_2)}) \varepsilon (a_{g1}, a_{g2}, \ldots, a_{gm}) \times (a_{k1}, a_{k2},$$

$$\ldots, a_{km}); \mu_C : (a_{gj} \times a_{kj}) \longrightarrow [0, 1] \qquad (4.21)$$

where $X_{ig}^{(h_1)}$ will be said to support $X_{ik}^{(h_2)}$ if $h_1 < h_2$, and μ_C is an estimate of the degree of support. This could obviously be extended to several actions:

$$DC(((X_{i1}^{(h_1)}, X_{i2}^{(h_1)}, \ldots, X_{ik}^{(h_1)}) \rightarrow X_{ik}^{(h_2)}), \mu_{C_1}^{(1)}, \mu_{C_2}^{(1)}, \ldots, \mu_{C_k}^{(1)}), \text{ or} \qquad (4.22)$$

$$DC(((X_{ig}^{(h_1)}) \rightarrow (X_{i1}^{(h_2)}, X_{i2}^{(h_2)}, \ldots, X_{ik}^{(h_2)}) \mu_{C_1}^{(2)}, \mu_{C_2}^{(2)}, \ldots, \mu_{C_k}^{(2)}), \qquad (4.23)$$

for example, and also to several hierarchical levels: $h_1, h_2 \varepsilon [0, 1, \ldots, \overset{*}{h}-1, \overset{*}{h}]$. This relation corresponds to (4.20) i; the relation corresponding to (4.20) ii can then be given the following form:

$$DB((X_{ig}^{(h_1)}, X_{ik}^{(h_2)}), \mu_B) \sqsubseteq \{ (X_{ig}^{(h_1)}, X_{ik}^{(h_2)}) \varepsilon (a_{g1}, a_{g2}, \ldots, a_{gm}) \times (a_{k1}, a_{k2}, \ldots, a_{km}); \ \mu_B : (a_{gj} \times a_{kj}) \rightarrow [0, 1] \} \quad (4.24)$$

where $h_1 = h_2$, and μ_B is an estimate of the degree of simultaneity; as in the case of μ_C it should be observed that μ_B is defined for the same dimension in each pair of attributes. Also this relation can be extended to several actions, which, however, should now be of the same hierarchical level:

$$DB((X_{i1}^{(h_1)}, X_{i2}^{(h_1)}, \ldots, X_{ik}^{(h_1)}), \mu_{B_1}, \mu_{B_2}, \ldots, \mu_{B_k}) \quad (4.25)$$

if the "degree of simultaneity" is the same for all the actions $X_{ik}^{(h_1)}$, the membership functions μ_{B_k} (k = 1, ..., k) are replaced by μ_B. The DB-relation can also be used to formulate the "simultaneity" of an action and an external event:

$$DB_E((X_{ik}^{(h_1)}, Y_{jv}^{(h_1)}), \mu_{BE}) \quad (4.26)$$

or several actions and external events:

$$DB_E((X_{i1}^{(h_1)}, X_{i2}^{(h_1)}, \ldots, X_{ik}^{(h_1)}; Y_{j1}^{(h_1)}, Y_{j2}^{(h_1)}, \ldots, Y_{jv}^{(h_1)}), \mu_{BE_1}, \mu_{BE_2}, \ldots, \mu_{BE_k}) \quad (4.27)$$

where we also could have various combinations of activities vs one external event, several external events, etc, whereby the membership functions should cover these combinations (this aspect is omitted in order to save space). As in (4.25) one μ_{BE} could replace the series $\mu_{BE}, \mu_{BE}, \ldots, \mu_{BE}$; the attribute sets covering activities and external events were assumed to represent the same level of hierarchy in order to avoid the need for transformations of attribute sets.

If three actions $X_{i1}^{(h_1)}$, $X_{i2}^{(h_1)}$ and $X_{i1}^{(h_2)}$, where $h_1 < h_2$, are covered by a DB- and DC-relation, such that the actions form an interlinked whole, they can be said to form a system (cf [7]); as this is the smallest entity formed by the elements we have introduced, it can be referred to as an elementary system (if $h_2 = 1$, it could be labelled a 1-level, elementary system). Two elementary systems form a subsystem (which is labelled with the highest h-value of the elementary systems) if at least one pair of actions, one from each elementary system, is interlinked through either a DB- or DC-relation; if more than two elementary systems form a sub-system there should be a "chain" of interlinked pairs of actions between the systems.

If all the actions of $\mathcal{X}_i$ are interlinked through DB- and DC-relations, in such a way that each corresponding attribute set is linked to every other attribute set, either directly or indirectly, $\mathcal{X}_i$ is a system (cf [7]); moreover, it is a hierarchical, multilevel fuzzy system. It is fuzzy, because it is formed by fuzzy relations between fuzzy sets (cf [54]).

The problem of distinguishing between a system and its environment could here be tackled with the help of the fuzzy DB_E-relations, either so that they delimit the environment, or so that external activities for which $\mu_{BE} > \alpha$, where α is a chosen parameter, are included in the system.

If there exist membership functions, such that $\mathcal{X} = \{ (\mathcal{X}_1, \mu_{12}), (\mathcal{X}_2, \mu_{23}), \ldots, (\mathcal{X}_{n-1}, \mu_{(n-1)n}), (\mathcal{X}_n, \mu_n)\}$ i.e. the systems $\mathcal{X}_i$ are interlinked over the interval $[t_1, t_n]$, $\mathcal{X}$ is said to form a fuzzy, dynamic system.

As can be seen from this discussion, the introduction of a (fuzzy) systems approach requires a vast apparatus of concepts; the intuitive meaning of actions and relations is clear in everyday language, but we need all the formulae (4.1) - (4.27) to create the necessary tools for modelling purposes.

With the systems framework thus established, it remains to find out how it could be applied to the MCDM-area; the systems framework was, of course, adapted to a management context, but it remains to be seen how a set of objectives could be formulated in systems terminology:

Let us now assume that there is given a set of objectives G (the general case; cf section 1.3), and that it is the task of DM to establish the necessary and sufficient requirements for attaining all the objectives of G, either in $[t_1, t_n]$, or at least by t_n. The set G may be formulated by DM, at least in part, or given to him as a responsibility.

An objective will here be taken to be a subset of the fuzzy attribute sets describing (i) one or several actions, (ii) one or several external events, or (iii) some combination of actions and external events. If we make use of the concepts we introduced in the previous section this concept may be formulated as follows,

$$\mathbf{G}_1 = \{ G_{11}, G_{12}, \ldots, G_{1k} \}, \text{ i.e. the goal set } G_1, \text{ at some } t_1 \in [t_1, t_n] \quad (4.28)$$

is described by k attribute sets, and the set G of objectives by the family,

$$\mathbf{G} = \{ \mathbf{G}_1, \mathbf{G}_2, \ldots, \mathbf{G}_l \}, \text{ for the interval } [t_1, t_n] \quad (4.29)$$

Then we have for $\mathbf{G}_1$,

$$\mathbf{G}_1 = \{ (g_{1km} \mid g_{1km} \sqsubseteq G_{1k}, \ (\forall k(\forall m)) \}, \text{ where} \quad (4.30)$$

$$g_{1km} = \{ a_{ikm}, \mu_g(a_{ikm})\}, \forall m, \text{ where } a_{ikm} \in A_{ik}, \text{ or} \quad (4.31)$$

$$g_{1km} = \{ a_{i1m} \times a_{i2m}, \mu_g(a_{i1m}, a_{i2m})\}, \forall m, \text{ or for } (a_{i1m} \times a_{i2m} \times \ldots \times a_{ikm}), \quad (4.32)$$

$$g_{1km}^{(h)} = \{ a_{ikm}^{(h)}, \mu_g(a_{ikm}^{(h)})\}, \forall m, \forall h \quad (4.33)$$

$$g_{1km}^{(h_2)} = \{ a_{ikm}^{(h_1)} \times a_{ikm}^{(h_2)}, \ \mu_g(a_{ikm}^{(h_1)}, a_{ikm}^{(h_2)})\}, \forall m, (h_1 < h_2) \in H, \quad (4.34)$$

which could be extended to several actions, and several hierarchical levels. In the latter case we could have,

$$\mathbf{G}_1 = \{ G_{1k}^{(h)}\}, \text{ for } (h = 0, 1, \ldots, h^*-1, h^*), h \in H \text{ and } k = 1, \ldots, k; \quad (4.35)$$

this means that the set $\mathbf{G}_1$ would have a hierarchical structure, corresponding to that of $\mathbf{X}_i$. As pointed out above, we could also have,

$$g_{1km} = \{ e_{jkm}, \mu_{ge}(e_{jkm})\}, \forall m; \quad (4.36)$$

or for two or more external events, cf (4.32),

$$g_{1km}^{(h)} = \{ e_{jkm}^{(h)}, \mu_{ge}(e_{jkm}^{(h)}\}, \forall m; \quad (4.37)$$

or for two or more hierarchical levels cf (4.34),

$$g_{1km} = \{ a_{ikm} \times e_{jkm}, \mu_g(a_{ikm}, e_{jkm})\}, \forall m, \quad (4.38)$$

which also could be done for two or more actions and external events, of the same or different hierarchical levels, if the μ_g membership functions are given an appropriate form.

The membership functions, denoted by μ_g and μ_{ge}, are given the following forms:

$$\mu_g(a_{ikm}) : (g_{1km} \sqsubseteq a_{ikm}) \rightarrow [0, 1], \forall m \tag{4.39}$$

$$\mu_{ge}(e_{jkm}) : (g_{1km} \sqsubseteq e_{jkm}) \rightarrow [0, 1], \forall m \tag{4.40}$$

$$\mu_g(a_{ikm}, e_{jkm}) : (g_{1km} \sqsubseteq a_{ikm} \times e_{jkm}) \rightarrow [0, 1], \forall m \tag{4.41}$$

which could be developed into more specific forms if we have several actions and external events, which may be organized on one or more hierarchical levels. The membership functions give the degree to which an objective g_{1km} is a subset of one or more activities and/or one or more external events, and this is carried out for all the m dimensions we gave an attribute set.

From the definitions in (4.28) - (4.41) we may deduce that the concept we have introduced has the following properties:

i. an objective is formulated in the same dimensions, and with the same attributes, as actions and external events,
ii. an objective is a fuzzy set; the corresponding membership function shows the degree (for all dimensions) to which an objective is a subset of activities and/or external events,
iii. an objective may be associated with a hierarchical level; a set of objectives may be organized hierarchically,
iv. as the corresponding activities and external events are interlinked by DB-, DB_E- and DC-relations, a set of objectives will also have the properties of "being simultaneous" or "supporting/being supported by" each other. (4.42)

If there exist appropriate membership functions, we may - analogously with $\mathbf{X}$ - obtain a family $\mathbf{G} = \{(\mathbf{G}_1, \mu_{12}^{(g)}), (\mathbf{G}_2, \mu_{23}^{(g)}), \ldots, (\mathbf{G}_{n-1}, \mu_{(n-1)n}^{(g)}), (\mathbf{G}_n)\}$, i.e. the sets $\mathbf{G}_1$ of objectives are interlinked over the interval $[t_1, t_n]$. Then there are different forms for attainment with respect to $\mathbf{G}$:

i. all the objectives are attained at t_1, and stay attained for $[t_1, t_n]$,
ii. all the objectives are attained simultaneously at some $t_i \in [t_1, t_n]$,
iii. all the objectives have been attained at least once by t_n,
iv. all the objectives have been attained, to some degree, at least once by t_n. (4.43)

These forms of attainment seem to suggest, that it might be worthwhile to develop algorithms which do not aim at a traditional, simultaneous attainment of all the objectives in an MCDM-problem. One of the obstacles for such an endeavour has been the lack of an operational conceptual framework; the outlined hierarchical fuzzy systems approach may be useful for removing that obstacle.

We may then conclude that this way of treating objectives is conceptually more powerful than the objective functions and the constraints of the MOLP- and F-MOLP approaches. There are several reasons for this - those listed in (4.42)i-iv - but an essential result is that we could have different forms of attainment of an objective (cf (4.43)i-iv), which means that an MCDM-problem could be solved in various ways. With the MOLP- and F-MOLP models we try to find alternative courses of action which result in simultaneous attainment (maybe to some degree in F-MOLP) of all the objectives - (4.43) suggests that simultaneous attainment may not be necessary, which could open up new possibilities for algorithms.

Although the systems approach seems to have useful properties as a conceptual framework, it has a decisive drawback: there are no available algorithmic interpretations of the systems approach which could transform (4.1)-(4.43) into useful tools for problem-solving and decision-making. The systems approach is a great instrument for describing insight on an abstract level, but not for selecting alternative courses of action in order to resolve an MCDM-problem.

In relation to the obstacles described in the case text (cf section 1.3) we have the following results:

- Re (1.1) with the systems approach it is possible to describe how objectives <u>could</u> be attained, not how they <u>are</u> attained;
- Re (1.2) the systems concept introduced was given a hierarchical structure, i.e. it has the necessary properties as a framework for composition/decomposition;
- Re (1.3) such a scheme cannot be constructed without an algorithm operationalising the systems concept;
- Re (1.4) interdependence of the objectives was explicitly introduced as a conceptual feature; it can be handled with DB-, DB_E- and DC-relations, but only on an abstract level;
- Re (1.5) different degrees of attainment for the objectives is another feature explicitly introduced in the systems approach; conceptually this feature is handled with membership functions; again the operations are valid only on an abstract level;

Then we may conclude that the systems approach may be useful as an abstract and theoretical framework, but that it should be developed considerably before it will have any practical influence in the MCDM-area. The systems approach belongs to the two "cubes" systems research - adaptation/development objectives - analytic/ search-learning means, mainly because it helps in formulating and describing insight; a decision-maker benefits more from insight for adaptation or development objectives - which may be rather abstract - than for operations objectives, which should be fairly explicit. Regarding our four steps for a conceptual delimitation of the MCDM-area, the systems approach is clearly the most liberal: (i) the family **A** is intended to cover all possible alternatives of action; (ii) the systems concept is hierarchical, which allows different levels of decision-making activity to be represented; (iii) there are no explicit tools for multiple-criteria problem-solving; (iv) there are no algorithms available which could turn the systems approach into a model which facilititates problem-solving and decision-making. Only for strategic activities might there be some use for a systems approach of the kind we have introduced here, i.e. the systems approach represents level (i) modelling.

5. SUMMARY AND CONCLUSION

We have discussed some features of a methodology for dealing with multiple-criteria problems at some length. We started by carrying out a few steps towards conceptualizing the MCDM-area, and formulated a generalized case as an example and a framework for a comparison of three different methodologies - or approaches - for handling multiple-criteria problems. These approaches were (i) multiple-objective linear programming, (ii) fuzzy multiple-objective linear-programming and (iii) a (fuzzy) systems approach.

We found that MOLP (methodology (i)) is a useful tool for handling situations with many objectives, and needs for a composition/decomposition type of assessment and evaluation of the objectives; MOLP cannot, however, handle conflicts, advanced forms of interdependence among the objectives, or partial attainment of the objectives.

We found that F-MOLP (methodology (ii)) also handles situations with many objectives, and could be used for handling composition/decomposition types of assessment and evaluation of the objectives; F-MOLP was developed for handling advanced forms of interdependence among the objectives, and can handle conflicts; F-MOLP is also equipped for handling partial attainment of the objectives.

We found, finally, that the systems approach (methodology (iii)) is useful only as a means for formulating insight; it is not very practical as a tool for multiple-criteria problem-solving. The systems approach, however, revealed that there could be various forms of attainment of a set of objectives, which provides some useful hints for developing algorithms in the MCDM-area.

We may therefore conclude that none of the studied three methodologies is decisevely better than the two others, that they serve partially different purposes, and that all of them should be developed further.

6. REFERENCES

1 Ackoff, Russell L. Beyond Problem Solving, General Systems, Vol XIX, 1974.

2 Anthony, Robert N. Planning and Control Systems. A Framework for Analysis, Division of Research, Harvard Business School, Boston 1965.

3 Belenson, S.M. and K.C. Kapur An algorithm for solving multicriteria linear programming problems with examples, Oper.Res. Quarterly, vol. 24, no. 1.

4 Bellman, R.E. and L.A. Zadeh Decision-making in a fuzzy environment, Management Sci. 17, 1970, 141-164.

5 Carlsson, C. An approach to adaptive, multigoal control using fuzzy automata, in Advances in Operations Research, Roubens, Ed. Proc. of EURO II. Amsterdam: North-Holland Publ. Co., 1977.

6 Carlsson, C. Adaptive multigoal control. On the Principles for Problem Solving in a Complex Environment, Ph.D. dissertation (in Swedish), Åbo 1977.

7 Carlsson, C. A system of problems and how to deal with it, presented at 4th Int. Congress of Cybern. and Syst., Amsterdam, 1978.

8 Carlsson, C. — Linking MP Models in a Systems Framework, IEEE Transactions, Vol SMC-9, No. 12, 1979.

9 Carlsson, C. — An Approach to Fuzzy, Dynamic Systems Modelling, Actes Table Ronde, CNRS sur le Flou, Lyon 1980.

10 Carlsson, C. - A. Törn - M. Zeleny, eds. — Multiple Criteria Decision Making: Selected Case Studies, McGraw-Hill, New York, 1981.

11 Carlsson, C. — Solving Mr Oakes' plywood production problem with a fuzzy MOLP-method, in: C. Carlsson et al., Eds., Multiple Criteria Decision Making: Selected Case Studies, McGraw-Hill, New York, 1981.

12 Carlsson, C. — Solving ill-structured problems through well-structured fuzzy programming, in J.P. Brans, Ed., Operational Research '81, North Holland, Amsterdam, 1981.

13 Carlsson, C. — Tackling an MCDM-Problem with Some Results from Fuzzy Set Theory, European Journal of Operational Research, July 1982.

14 Carlsson, C. — Complex Management Problems and a Systems Concept: An Adaptation and Application of Structure Systems, Progress in Cybernetics and Systems Research, Vol VIII, Hemisphere Publ. Corp., Washington 1982.

15 Charnes, A. - W.W. Cooper et al. — Explicit solutions in convex goal programming, Management Sci., vol. 22, no. 4., 1975.

16 Charnes, A. - W.W. Cooper — Goal programming and multiple objective optimizations, Management Science Research Rep. 381, Univ. Texas. Nov. 1975.

17 Cochrane, J.L. - M. Zeleny, Eds., Multiple Criteria Decision Making, University of South Carolina Press, Columbia, 1973.

18 Dubois, D. - H. Prade New result about properties and semantics of fuzzy set - theoretic operators, in: P.P. Wang and S.K. Chang, Eds., Fuzzy Sets, Plenum, New York, 1980.

19 Dubois, D. - H. Prade Fuzzy Sets and Systems: Theory and Applications, Academic Press, New York, 1980.

20 Geoffrion, A.M. Proper efficiency and theory of vector maximization, J. Mathematical Analysis and Applications, vol 22, 1968.

21 Gupta, M.M. - G.N. Saridis - B.R. Gaines, eds. Fuzzy Automata and Decision Processes, North-Holland, New York, 1977.

22 Isermann, H., The enumeration of the set of all efficient solutions for a linear multiple objective program, Oper. Res. Quarterly, vol. 28. no. 3, 1977.

23 Johnsen, Erik Teorien om ledelse, Nyt Nordisk Forlag, København, 1975.

24 Kalman, R., - N. De Claris, ed. Aspects of Network and Systems Theory, Holt, Rineharts and Winston, New York, 1971.

25 Kornbluth, J.S.H. Duality, indifference and sensitivity analysis in multiple objective linear programming, Oper. Res. Quarterly, vol. 25. no. 4, 1974.

26 Lee, S.M. Goal Programming for Decision Analysis, Philadelphia: Auerbach Publ., 1972.

27 Leung, Y. A fuzzy set procedure for project selection with hierarchical objectives, in: P.P. Wang and S.K. Chang, Eds., Fuzzy Sets, Plenum, New York, 1980.

28 Lientz, B.P. — On time dependent fuzzy sets, Information Sci. 4, 1972, 367-376.

29 MacCrimmon, K.R. — An overview of multiple, objective decision making, in: J.L. Cochrane and M. Zeleny, Eds., Multiple Criteria Decision Making (University of South Carolina Press, Columbia, 1973.

30 Negoita, C.V. - D.A. Ralescu — Applications of Fuzzy Sets to Systems Analysis, ISR 11, Birkhäuser Verlag, Basel 1975.

31 Negoita, C.V. - D.A. Ralescu — On fuzzy optimization, Kybernetes 6, 1977, 193-195.

32 Negoita, C.V. — Management Applications of System Theory, ISR 57, Birkhäuser Verlag, Basel 1979.

33 Negoita, C.V. — On the Applications of Fuzzy Sets in System Analysis, Intervenant, CNRS Round Table of Fuzzy Sets, Lyon 1980.

34 Negoita, C.V. — Fuzzy Systems, Abacus Press, Singapore 1981.

35 Orlovsky, S.A. — On formalization of a general fuzzy mathematical problem, Fuzzy Sets Systems 3, 1980, 311-321.

36 Philip, J. — Algorithms for the vector maximization problem, Mathematical programming, vol. 2, 1972.

37 Pollatschek, M.A. — Hierarchical systems and fuzzy-set theory, Kybernetes 6, 1977, 147-151.

38 Prade, H.M. — Operations research with fuzzy data, in: P.P. Wang and S.K. Chang, Eds., Fuzzy Sets, Plenum, New York, 1980.

39 Sommer, G., — Bayes-Entscheidungen bei unscharfer Problembeschreibung, European University Studies, Peter D. Lang, Frankfurt am Main, 1980.

40 Simon, H.A. The Organization of Complex Systems, in: Pattee, H.H. (ed.): Hierarchy Theory, George Braziller, New York 1973.

41 Simon, H.A. Rational decision making in business organizations, Amer. Econom. Rev. 69, 1979, 493-513.

42 Sugeno, M. - T. Terano Analytical Representation of Fuzzy Systems, in: Gupta-Saridis-Gaines (ed.): Fuzzy Automata and Decision Processes. North Holland, New York, 1977.

43 Sugeno, M. On Structured Set of Systems, Report No. 5, The Working Group on Fuzzy Systems, Tokyo, Dec. 1977.

44 Takeda, E. - T. Nishida Multiple criteria decision problems with fuzzy domination structures, Fuzzy Sets and Systems 3, 1980, 123-136.

45 Wang, P.P. - S.K. Chang, Eds. Fuzzy Sets, Plenum Press, New York, 1980.

46 Wiedey, G., - H.J. Zimmermann Media selection and fuzzy linear programming, J. Operational Res. Soc. 29, 1978, 1071-1084.

47 Yager, R.R. Mathematical programming with fuzzy constraints and a preference on the objective, Kybernetes 8, 1979, 285-291.

48 Yager, R.R. Decisions with ordinal preferences and importances, Kybernetes 9, 1980, 109-114.

49 Yager, R.R. Satisfaction and fuzzy decision functions, in: P.P. Wang and S.K. Chang, Eds., Fuzzy Sets, Plenum, New York, 1980.

50 Yu, P.L. Introduction to domination structures in multicriteria decision problems, in: J.L. Cochrane and M. Zeleny, Eds.,

Multiple Criteria Decision Making (University of South Carolina Press, Columbia, 1973.

51 Yu, P.L. — Linear multiparametric programming by multicriteria simplex method, Management Sci., vol. 23, no. 2, Oct. 1976.

52 Zadeh, L.A. — Fuzzy Sets and Systems, paper, 1965 Symposium on System Theory, Polytechnic Institute of Brooklyn.

53 Zadeh, L.A. — Probability Measures of Fuzzy Events, Journal of Mathematical Analysis and Applications, 23, 1968.

54 Zadeh, L.A. — Toward a Theory of Fuzzy Systems, in Kalman - De Claris (ed.): Aspects of Network and System Theory, Holt, Rineharts and Winston, New York, 1971.

55 Zadeh, L.A. — Outline of a New Approach to the Analysis of Complex Systems and Decision Process, in: J.L. Cochrane and M. Zeleny, Eds., Multiple Criteria Decision Making, University of South Carolina Press, Columbia, 1973.

56 Zeleny, M. — Compromise Programming, in: J.L. Cochrane and M. Zeleny, Eds., Multiple Criteria Decision Making, University of South Carolina Press, Columbia, 1973.

57 Zeleny, M. — Adaptive displacement of preferences in decision making, in TIMS Studies in Management Sciences 6, Amsterdam: North-Holland Publishing, 1977.

58 Zeleny, M. — Descriptive decision making and its applications, in: Applications of Management Science, Vol I, JAI Press, New York, 1980, 327-388.

59 Zeleny, M. — Multiple Criteria Decision Making, McGraw-Hill, New York, 1982.

THEORY AND PRACTICE OF
MULTIPLE CRITERIA DECISION MAKING
C. Carlsson and Y. Kochetkov (editors)

FUZZY CATASTROPHES IN NON-TRIVIAL DECISION-MAKING

V. DIMITROV
International Research Institute of Management Sciences
Schepkina str. 8, 129090 Moscow, USSR

ABSTRACT

Non-trivial decisions are decisions which lead to the discovery of new alternatives not previously known to the decision-maker. A model describing the process of making non-trivial decisions is developed; the model is based on Thom's two-parametric catastrophe. Due to the fuzziness of the considered parameters, the catastrophe is called fuzzy. Is is emphasized that the moment at which any upward jump in the two-parametric fuzzy catastrophe may take place is unpredictable, and this property explains the unpredictability of any act of generating non-trivial decisions. Is there any way to bring nearer the moment of making a new decision?
A positive answer to this question is given in the fuzzy-catastrophe framework presented.

1. INTRODUCTION

Repetition and Optimization - the main principles on which the modern decision-making is based.

According to the first principle, a decision taken in the case of an arbitrary problem situation s (with respect to a given goal) must repeat or be similar to the decision taken in the case of s_0, provided that s coincides with or is similar to s_0. Application of this principle (let us call it the Repetition Principle and denote it RP) is justified by a natural desire to minimize the efforts a decision-maker has to make in order to reach a decision with respect to given a problem situation s - why does the decision-maker try to create new decisions in the case of s, if a decision for s_0 is already available, and s is almost the same as s_0? The utility function concept widely used in different decision-making models is based on RP; it is enough to bear in mind the proof of Debreu's theorem of utility function existence; a central assumption preceding his proof concerns the so-called "continuation property of preferences": x_0Ry_0 implies xRy, where x and y are alternatives closed to x_0 and y_0 respectively and R is binary relation of weak preference. RP plays a fundamental role in probabilistic decision-making; all models explaining decision-making under risk and uncertainty use repetition as a main source of information. Applied to collective decision-making, RP takes the form of the omnipotent majority group choice rule: if a majority choses one and the same decision, i.e. if one and the same point of view is repeated by a majority of group's members, then this point of view is automatically accepted as a common decision for all the group, no matter which and how valuable are the decisions proposed by the individuals not included in the majority.

RP impedes the creative process of making new decisions. Being subject to the yoke of RP, the decision-maker is involved in a continuous modification of old decisions to fit the new problem situation; such modification leads to trivial decisions only; a non-trivial decision arises as a result of a new "fresh" approach to the problem situation, being considered an approach free from any repetition. After some non-trivial decision has been created, a connection between it and some old decision may be established, but not as a result of any action of RP. RP will begin to act later, when the decision reached ceases to be new for subsequent problem situations.

According to the second principle - the Optimization Principle (OP), all decisions have to be made in an optimal way, i.e. satisfying the obligatory requirement for optimizing the values of criteria stated in advance. Since mathematics can still solve only a single-criterion optimization problem, while any real-life decision-making problem needs to take into consideration more than one criterion, the applications of OP lead either to oversimplification of the problem, i.e. transforming it into a singel-criterion problem (which results in much more harm than use) or to looking for the so-called "compromise optimum", satisfying all criteria up to certain degrees specified as optimal. But does it really make any sense to consider the agreed values of the criteria as optimal, and, by the same token, to interpret the compromise obtained as an optimal one? Taking into account the difficulty of multicriteria optimization, the term "optimal decision" is used with care and it is replaced by more or less fuzzy terms such as "quasi-optimal" or "good enough" or "decision satisfying the decision-maker up to a high enough degree", etc. However fuzzy the formulation of an optimal, from many criteria, decision may be, the way it is reached continues to follow the dictates of OP. This all-pervading principle places a very strong restriction on the decison-maker - before undertaking any search for the optimal decision, the set of all available decisions must be precisely determined; in other words, the decision-maker must know all the alternative ways that may lead to the chosen goal before analyzing which of them suits him best. Thus, OP interferes with the process of creating new (unknown in advance) alternative ways of reaching the goal. All that the decision-maker has to do is to look for some reasonable application of the Repetition Principle in order to choose the most preferable (according to the requirement of the Optimization Principle) alternative. But to choose an alternative among a set of alternatives specified, in advance using principles which dictate by force Repetition and Optimization, is nothing but a trivial decision, no matter how great the computational effort involved.

There must be an entirely different principle explaining the criterion of a new decision. This principle is implied by the Thom's classification theorem - a central theorem of catastrophe theory.

2. FUZZY CATASTROPHES

According to R. Thom - the founder of modern catastrophe theory [1] , almost every r-parametric family of smooth functions $R^n \rightarrow R$, for any n and $r < 4$, is structurally stable and equivalent * in the vicinity of any point to one of seven elementary catastrophes, each described by its own characteristic polynomial. These catastrophes represent seven stable patterns into which all possible changes occurring permanently in the objects of our three-dimensional world can be classified

* see footnote next page

If at least one of the parameters of the above family is determined in a fuzzy way, then the catastrophe, whose polynomial representation depends on this parameter, is called a <u>fuzzy catastrophe</u>. Fuzzy catastrophes are used for modelling the dynamics of human decision-making ability. This ability can be formally represented by a family of functions written as

$$F : R^n \times R^r \rightarrow R \tag{1}$$

where R^n is a n-dimensional space of variables over which the decision-maker (denoted by h) cannot exercise any control; R^r is a r-dimensional space of controlled parameters, and R is one-dimensional space of real numbers on which some integral (most general) estimate of the decision-making ability can be offered. Any exemplar of (1) represents some smooth function (i.e. function possessing partial derivatives of any order) f: $R^n \rightarrow R$ and is interpreted as the ability of the individual h to generate decisions under a fixed collection of values taken by the parameters in R^r; this ability is permanently realized through various decisions produced by h during all his reasonable life.

It is assumed that an act of decision generation can occur on (1) only at some of its equilibrium points, i.e. at points where

$$\frac{\partial f}{\partial x_i} = 0 \text{ for } i = 1, 2, \ldots, n$$

However, the actual realization of any decision generating process depends mainly upon the values taken by the controlled parameters. Two controlled parameters are considered below.

The first parameter characterizes the grade of awareness or knowledge possessed by h about the problem situation under which decisions are sought. The higher the value assigned to this parameter, the clearer the problem situation (let denote it by s) appears to h. The second parameter characterizes the strenght of adherence of attachment of h to the goal which has to be achieved. The higher the value assigned to this parameter, the more "passionately" h craves for the stated goal. How deeply does h know "the truth" about s, i.e. up to what degree are the

---

* The families F, G: $R^n \times R^r \rightarrow R$ are equivalent in the vicinity of a given point $(x_o, u_o) \varepsilon R^n \times R$, if in this vicinity two diffeomorphisms $e: R^r \rightarrow R$ and $y_u: R^r \rightarrow R$ for any $u \varepsilon R^r$, and a smooth mapping $z: R^r \rightarrow R$ can be determined, such that $G(x, u) = F(y_u(x), e(u)) + z(u)$ for all $(x, u) \varepsilon R^n \times R^r$ belonging to the vicinity of (x_o, u_o).

internal causes (regularities) acting behind s and determiningits external appearance known to h? How strongly does h strive towards the goal? The answers to these questions, with the exception of a few trivial cases, can be given only in a fuzzy way, i.e. by means of typical fuzzy expressions such as "very little", "little", "much", "not very much", "moderately", "strongly", "weakly", etc. Fuzzy set theory proposes a technique for translating such linguistic values into corresponding fuzzy subsets defined on the interval [0, 1] (see, for example [2, 3]), where in the case of the first parameter, 0 indicates complete absence of any information about s and 1 relates to an ideal case when s is completely known to h, and in the case of the second parameter, 0 indicates complete absence of any interest in the goal and 1 relates to an extremely strong attachment to it. Let the parameters be denoted by $\tilde{u}_1$ and $\tilde{u}_2$ respectively. Whether $\tilde{u}_1$ or $\tilde{u}_2$ will increase, decrease or remain on some unchangeable level depends entirely on h; in this sense $\tilde{u}_1$ and $\tilde{u}_2$ are considered to be controlled parameters.

Taking into account that the supports of all fuzzy subsets corresponding to the linquistic values assigned to the controlled parameters $\tilde{u}_1$ and $\tilde{u}_2$ belong to [0, 1] the family (1) can be rewritten as follows:

$$F : R^n \times [0, 1]^2 \rightarrow R \tag{2}$$

According to Thom, such a family is stable and equivalent to the socalled cusp catastrophe, having the form

$$F_{u_1, u_2}(x) = 1/4\, x^4 + 1/2\, x^2\tilde{u}_1 + x\tilde{u}_2 \tag{3}$$

As far as each fuzzy value of $\tilde{u}_i$, i = 1, 2 in (3) represents some fuzzy subset (denoted A_i), any non-fuzzy number from the support of A_i can be substituted in (3) However, it is necessary to know how great is the grade of membership of this fuzzy number in A_i. In other words, the fuzzy variant of the cusp catastrophe (3) is specified by the following four characteristics:

u_1^k, u_2^l - arbitrary non-fuzzy numbers from the supports of the fuzzy subsets A_1 and A_2 respectively; $u_1^k, u_2^l \in [0, 1]$;

$\mu_{A_1}(u_1^k)$, $\mu_{A_2}(u_2^l)$ - grades of membership of the non-fuzzy numbers u_1^k and u_2^l in the fuzzy subsets A_1 and A_2, respect., $\mu_{A_i}(u_1^k), \mu_{A_2}(u_2^l) \in [0,1]$.

The closer the above grades of membership to 1, the more precise and real the appearance of the fuzzy cusp catastrophe.

The set of all equilibrium points of (3) build a surface called a catastrophe manifold, shown in fig. 1 and defined by the following equation:

$$\frac{dF_{u_1,u_2}}{dx} = x^3 + x\,\tilde{u}_1 + \tilde{u}_2 = 0 \qquad (4)$$

Fig. 1 illustrates the process of formation of an abrupt change in the decision-making ability (d.m.a.) of h as a result of the gradual smooth changes of the values assigned to the parameters $\tilde{u}_1$ and $\tilde{u}_2$. When the magnitude of the grade of individual attachment to the stated goal exceeds a certain level, a further increase in $\tilde{u}_1$, i.e. a further extension of the knowledge about s, produces a sudden jump on the equilibrium surface of the d.m.a.; an upward jump occurs on A'P'. i.e. for values taken by $\tilde{u}_1$ and $\tilde{u}_2$ on the line AP (see fig. 1). On the other hand, a decrease in $\tilde{u}_1$ can produce a fall on the equilibrium surface of the d.m.a.; a downward jump occurs on B'P', i.e, for values taken by $\tilde{u}_1$ and $\tilde{u}_2$ on the line BP. (APB in fig. 1 forms the so-called bifurcation set of the catastrophe.)

3. NON-TRIVIAL DECISIONS THROUGH FUZZY CATASTROPHES

If the "energy" accumulated by the d.m.a. as a result of an upward (positive) jump taking place on the equilibrium surface (4) is "great enough", it could lead to the act of making a new decision; in this sense the cusp catastrophe (3) represents a potential generator of new decisions. Although made for the same problem situation (as all decisions produced on the equilibrium surface (4)), the new decision is not implied by the action either of RP or of OP. Let a denote a point on the catastrophe manifold corresponding to some new decision d * (see fig. 1). After d * is made, a connection between it and some of the decisions taken before the catastrophe jump under the dictate of RP can easily be established (line a*b' on fig. 1). With the establishment of such a connection, d* loses its property of being new. Later, at some further positive jump of d.m.a. another decision could be born anew; after that, yet another, etc. So the process of creating new deci-

---

* These three fuzzy subsets are given usually by standard membership functions, easily adjusted to the "taste" of any subject, i.e. to the way in which an individual understands the meaning of "large", "moderate" and "small" in any considered context.

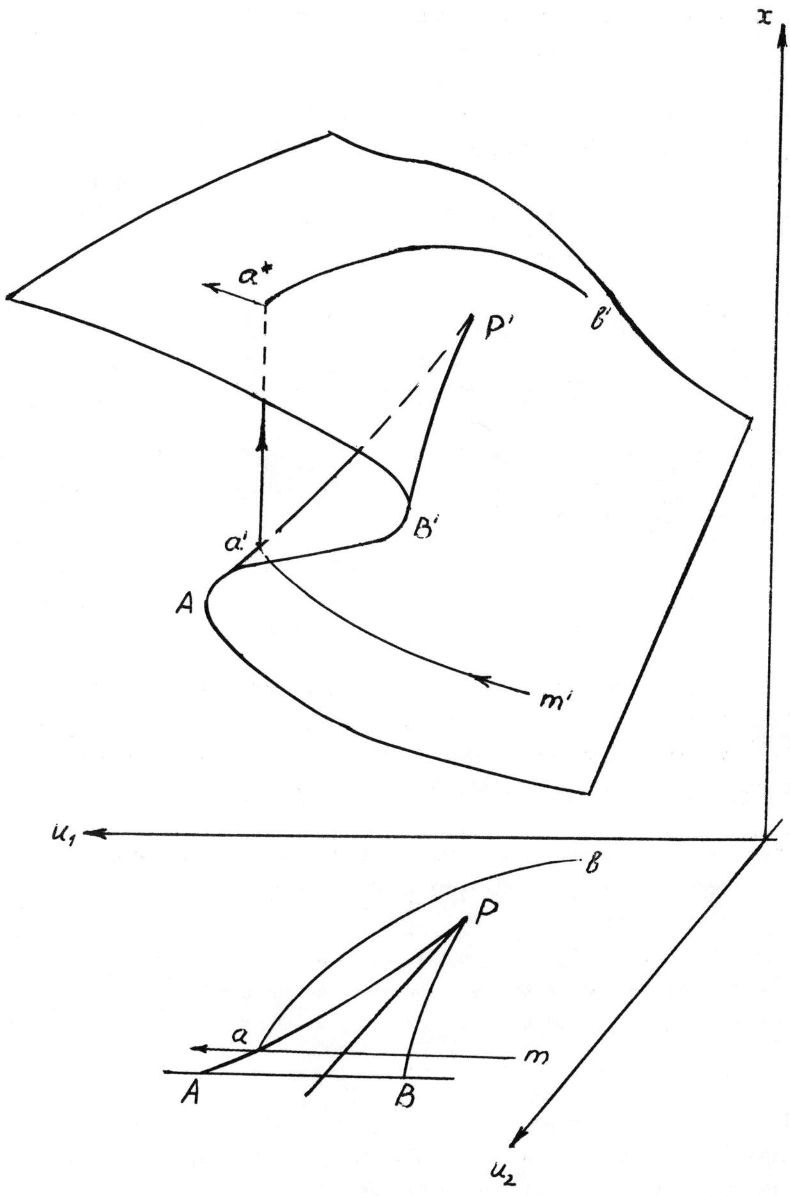

Fig. 1

sions continues until at least $\not\geq$ one human being able to learn ($\tilde{u}_1 \neq 0$) and to feel ($\tilde{u}_2 \neq 0$) is left on earth.

The continuous (smooth) character of the membership functions of the three basic fuzzy subsets (through which many other fuzzy modifications are easily obtained using the operations developed in fuzzy set theory): "large", "moderate" and "small" * defined on the interval [0, 1] for each of the parameters, leads to the following very important properties of the fuzzy cusp catastrophe:

(i) the moment at which any positive jump occurs in the fuzzy cusp catastrophe is unpredictable, and

(ii) negative jumps in the fuzzy cusp catastrophe are avoidable.

The first property confirms the unpredictability of every act of making a new decision; the second obliges the decision-maker to be alert and watchful when analyzing problem situations.

3. CONCLUSION

On the catastrophe manifolds corresponding to more complicated catastrophes and, therefore, more difficult to represent graphically (depending on three and more controlled variables), abrupt changes similar to the creative jump which occurs on the cusp catastrophe manifold are certainly present.

Does there exist any precept indicating how to bring nearer the moments of insight, i.e. the moments of making new non-trivial decisions? The answer to this question can easily be seen from fig. 1:

- by increasing u_1, i.e. by continuously deepening the knowledge about the true nature of the problems which the decision-maker encounters, and
- by keeping u_2 on a high enough level, i.e. by a strong desire to solve these problems.

By following these recommendations and with the ability to understand and feel the changes occurring permanently in life, the decision-maker could cease to be a simple repetitive and optimizing machine adjusted to generate a finite number of desires for accumulating more and more wealth, pleasures and weapons. Instead, he could become creative with the capacity to control the energy released through the insight catastrophes of his decision-making ability and to direct it to realize mankind's everlasting dream of happiness and perfection.

---

* see footnote - 2p

REFERENCES

1 Poston, E. - I. Stewart — Catastrophe theory and its applications, Pitman, 1978 *

2 Zadeh, L. — A theory of approximate reasoning, Mem.No UCB/ERL M77/58, Univ. of California, Berkeley.

3 Zadeh, L. — PRUF - A meaning representation language for natural language, Mem.No ERL-M77/61, Univ. of California, Berkeley.

* In this book a bibliography is given of all Thom's works and almost all publications on catastrophe theory up to 1977.

THEORY AND PRACTICE OF
MULTIPLE CRITERIA DECISION MAKING
C. Carlsson and Y. Kochetkov (editors)

COMPLEX ILL-STRUCTURED PROBLEMS IN MANAGEMENT SYSTEMS AND THEIR SOLUTION BY MAN

S.V. KHAYNISH, A.G. VLASOV

International Research Institute for Management Sciences
Shepkina Street 8, Moscow 129090 USSR

ABSTRACT

This paper classifies problems encountered in management systems. Depending on the nature of the problems, they are classified as simple or complex and well or ill-structured. Complex ill-structured problems are encountered in management systems quite extensively. A formal description is suggested for stating a complex ill-structured problem; for its solution descriptive models of the problem-solver's behaviour are used which represent the solution process as a multi-stage procedure. The resultant procedure can be used in developing interactive systems which adapt to the actual problem-solver's behaviour both for the improvement of solution processes and the training of managers.

1. CLASSIFICATION OF PROBLEMS TO BE SOLVED IN ORGANIZATIONAL SYSTEMS

Let us consider the specifics of the processes involved in solving problems in organizational systems. First some related concepts must be introduced [1].

An organization (organizational system) is a system where major components are man and his activity in achieving a global objective (or a set of objectives).

A global objective is the attainment (maintenance) of the maximum effectiveness of the organization's functioning in terms of a certain global criterion (or set of criteria).

An organization can be viewed as a combination of two sub-systems, one being the management system and the other the manufacturing process.

Management systems are those which handle a factory, an industrial plant, an industrial sector, state planning and supply committees, etc.

Man's activity in organizational management systems involves solving various problems such as supply, planning, forecasting, ordering, etc.

The problems to be tackled in organizational management systems are classified according to the nature of their description.

Depending on the degree with which its description is formalized, the problem is either ill-structured or well-structured.

The problem is defined as ill-structured if in its description [3, 8]:
- qualitative features prevail;
- the representation is implicit;
- quantities are not specified or fixed in advance.

The problem complexity is measured in terms of several characteristics of its description [4]:
- dimension;
- non-linearity;
- stochasticity;
- dynamism;
- interdependence.

Depending on the value of these indices the problems are classified as simple or complex.

In summary, the problem can be classified as follows (Fig. 1)

Problem			
well-structured		ill-structured	
simple	complex	simple	complex

Fig. 1. Classification of Problems To Be Tackled in Organizations

The features of many problems which arise in management systems are reasonably similar to those of an complex ill-structured problem.

The design of practicable formal or heuristic methods for solving such problems remains a largely unexplored field at present. However, in actual management the human problem-solver often faces such problems and in many cases copes with them quite satisfactorily. Attempts to use formal methods and present-day computing technology to improve the solution of such problems have, however, met with considerable difficulty. Let us consider two such difficulties. When the problem is ill-structured but modelled in a well-structured description, the actual situation is far from adequately represented. As a result, the problem-solver finds it difficult to use this model. On the other hand, even if all necessary process functioning laws have been explored, the statement of the problem is a good representation of the real situation and so a solution algorithm, often interactive, is suggested, the problem-solver may nevertheless reject it because it is different from what he is used to and so the problem-solver fears "being out of his depth".

Complex ill-structured problems are quite widespread in management systems and methods for their solution would be welcome.

2. STATEMENT OF A COMPLEX ILL-STRUCTURED PROBLEM

Schematically many problems which are solved in management systems can be represented as follows (Fig. 2)

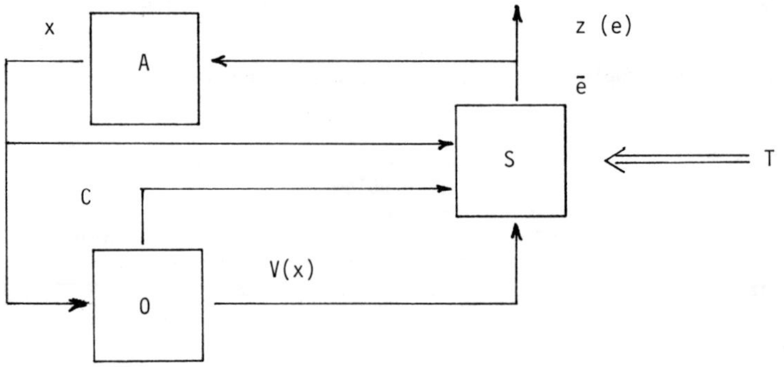

Fig. 2. Flowchart of a Problem to Be Resolved in an Organization

Here

0 - process description;
S - description of problem-solver's system of preferences;
A - description of the solution algorithm;
x - control;
V - process features dependent on x;
C - process features indenpendent of x;
e - sets of estimates of V, x, and C;
z - effectiveness;
T - objective.

Consequently, description of the problem D incorporates the following components: 0, S, A, T.

D = (0, S, A, T)

The problem is solved when the objective T is reached, giving the highest efficiency z through specifying the "best" control x.

The description of a complex ill-structured problem is influenced by the fact that, when starting to solve it, the problem-solver does not necessarily know in a general case what features of the process he will use in its solution, i.e. the number of the features may be high and not fixed in advance. Furthermore, the problem-solver may no be fully aware of his own system of preferences; consequently, it is possible to speak only of the existence of a certain system of preferences on the set of feature estimates rather than of the effectiveness function determined on the same set. Moreover, the problem-solver does not, in a general case, have sufficient knowledge about the set of admissible controls x or a clear idea of the "best" control. The "best" control is therefore determined (generated) by the problem-solver and not necessarily chosen from a set specified in advance [6]. These characteristics of a complex ill-structured problem should be represented in its statement.

The term problem-solver differs from decision-maker, which is often used in the literature on decision-making, and has been introduced to emphasize the fact that the manager's activity is not confined to making decisions which involve cilecting or ordering options; rather he has also to acquire the information for needed to make decisions and to formulate the various elements of the problem.

What follows is a version of the description and statement of a complex ill-structured problem.

The process is described in terms of a set of features $K = (K_1, K_2, \ldots)$. whose estimates form on certain scales a set E of totalities of feature estimate values $(E = E_1 x E_2 x \ldots)$. Elements $\bar{e}$ of the set E $(\bar{e} \in E)$ depend on a general case on the control x : $\bar{e} = \bar{e}(x)$. In solving the problem the control is determined in such a way as to maximize the effectiveness determined on the set E. This condition presupposes the existence of preference relations on the set E.

Let us assume that on the set E a binary relation R is introduced which is interpreted as - "no less preferable than". R exhibits reflexivity. It can express other binary relations which can be determined on E.

Let $\bar{e}_1, \bar{e}_m \in E$; then

P - is the strict preference relation

$$\bar{e}_1 P \bar{e}_m = \bar{e}_1 R \bar{e}_m \wedge \urcorner (\bar{e}_m R \bar{e}_1)$$

N - is an incomparability relation

$$\bar{e}_1 N \bar{e}_m = \urcorner (\bar{e}_1 R \bar{e}_m) \wedge \urcorner (\bar{e}_m R \bar{e}_1)$$

By definition N is symmetrical and P is antireflexive.

Let us refer to the subset $E_+ \sqsubset E$ as the set of weakly maximal elements of the set E [9] if

$$\forall \bar{e}_l \in E_+, \forall \bar{e}_m \in E \setminus E_+, (\bar{e}_l\ P\ \bar{e}_m \vee \bar{e}_l\ N\ \bar{e}_m) \wedge$$

$$\wedge\ (\neg \exists\ \bar{e}_n \in E_+ : \forall \bar{e}_p \in E \setminus E_+, \bar{e}_n\ N\ \bar{e}_p)$$

From this definition it follows that certain elements of E_+ are incomparable with others but not with all elements of $E \setminus E_+$.

I should be noted that E_+ can be identified from E in different ways [9].

To solve the problem it is necessary , in a general case, to determine the set of "best" controls X_+ which lead to the best set of feature estimate values E_+, "best" that is in the sense of effectiveness.

Consequently, the problem can be formulated as follows:

It is required to find

$$X_+ : \forall x \in X_+, \bar{e}(x) \in E_+, E_+ \sqsubset E.$$

The problem can be best solved through "successive identification of preferences simultaneously with investigation of the admissible set of controls" [7] . In compliance with this approach the problem is solved in a multi-stage procedure; at each stage both the statement of the problem and the set of "best" controls are updated. The problem-solver is in this case the information medium.

To solve the problem it is necessary to have at each stage:

- a description of the process including:
1) description of the set K;
2) description of the set E;
3) description of the set X_+;
4) description of the elements $x \in X_+$.
- a description of the problem-solver's system of preferences including:
description of the set E_+.
- a description of problem solution algorithms including:
1) description of the algorithm for determining E_+ ;
2) description of the algorithm for determing X_+.

Let us see what characteristics are typical of complex ill-structured problems:

1. The set of features K which describe the process are not necessarily explicitly given or fixed in advance. Therefore the number of elements of K can be high and their composition unknown in advance.

In a general case the set K may consist of a set of elements which are dependent on x - K_{var}, a set of elements which are independent of x - K_{const}, and a set of elements which coincide with x - K_x.

$$K = K_{var} \sqcup K_{const} \sqcup K_x$$

2. The scales of measurement of the features contained in the set K may be of an arbitrary nature. Consequently, components of elements $\bar{e}$ in the set E can be of either a quantitative or qualitative nature.

The dependence $\bar{e}(x)$ is not necessarily given explicitly and is generally of a complex, non-linear, stochastic, dynamic nature.

3. Description of the set X_+ is not necessarily explicitly specified or fixed in advance. Consequently, the number of elements of X_+ may be high and their composition unknown in advance.

4. In a description of the control $x \in X_+$ qualitative features may be prevalent.

5. In the set of feature estimate values E_+ "best" from the problem-solver's views of effectiveness is not necessarily specified explicitly or fixed in advance. This is caused by the complex nature of both the very concept of effectiveness and the problem-solver's system of preferences of which he is not usually fully aware.

6. The algorithms for determining the set of the "best" values of feature estimates E_+ and the set of the "best" controls X_+ are not necessarily specified explicitly or fixed in advance. Furthermore, these algorithms should in a general case ensure determination (generation) of E_+ and X_+ rather than their choice from certain fixed sets.

3. POSSIBLE METHODS FOR SOLVING COMPLEX ILL-STRUCTURED PROBLEMS BY USING THE DESCRIPTIVE APPROACH

At present there are no formal or heuristic methods for solving complex ill-structured problems as stated above that would work in real life. Since the problem-solver occupies a key position in the solution process as the store of necessary information, he should contribute to solving the problem, in particular, with an interactive system. The latter should be built around a descriptive model representing the behaviour of a skilled and experienced problem-solver. Then the interactive system would adapt to the actual problem-solver's behaviour and the problem would be effectively solved.

Most descriptive models of a problem-solver's behaviour [9] describe his behaviour only in developing the decision rules, in other words, algorithms for determining E_+ and X_+ in the above statement of the problem. The statement of the problem is assumed to be explicit and fixed in advance. In the light of the above remarks on the nature of the description of a complex ill-structured problem the descriptive model should be built for the process of solving the problem as a whole.

The authors have developed such descriptive models for certain problems in an organization such as object ordering, resource allocation and planning [2,4,10,11].

Let us take a look at a possible descriptive model of a problem-solver's behaviour in solving a complex ill-structured problem in the above statement.

The model of a problem-solver's behaviour was built on the knowledge of the literature, observations, and analysis of the behaviour of skilled and experienced problem-solvers in tackling specific planning and managerial tasks in organizations. The "bounded rationality" concept [5] was used, whereby the problem-solver perceives the problem he faces only to a certain extent. When this extent is surpassed, the problem-solver replaces the problem with a simplified model which retains the basic properties of the problem and so permits the problem-solver to stay within the framework of "rational", or logically motivated, behaviour. In solving the problem he successively breaks down the problem into sub-problems of a complexity limited to a certain level.

What follows is a brief description of the descriptive model of a problem-solver's behaviour at the i-th stage of the multi-stage procedure of problem solution.

The number of set features $K = (K_1, K_2, \ldots)$ is high and their composition is unknown in advance. With the set K known the problem-solver determines its certain subset $K_\Sigma = (K_{\Sigma 1}, K_{\Sigma 2}, \ldots)$, $(K_\Sigma \sqsubset K)$. The set K_Σ is a set of chosen features. These are effectiveness criteria which the problem-solver uses at the stage.

The number of criteria of the set K_Σ can in a general case be also high and their composition unknown in advance. Let E_Σ denote the set of totalities of values for scales of criteria for the set K_Σ

$$E_\Sigma = E_{\Sigma 1} \times E_{\Sigma 2} \times \ldots$$

Because the problem-solver cannot deal with a large number of criteria, he determines a finite subset $K_I = (k_{I1}, k_{I2}, \ldots k_{In})$, $(K_I \sqsubset K_\Sigma)$ in the set K_Σ. The set K_I is a most important set of criteria in the problem-solver's view. The number of criteria in the set K_I is low and their composition fixed.

Let us note that in a general case

$$K_I = K_{Ivar} \sqcup K_{Iconst} \sqcup K_{Ix}$$

Criteria values for the set K_I on appropriate scales make up a set E_I of totalities of values for criteria

$$E_I = E_{I1} \times E_{I2} \times \ldots \times E_{In}$$

Let $\bar{e}_I$ denote an element of the set E_I $(\bar{e}_I \in E_I)$. With due regard for the above remark on the nature of K_I it can be represented as

$$E_I = E_{Ivar} \times E_{Iconst} \times E_{Ix}$$

where E_{Ivar} - set of totalities of values for criteria K_{Ivar};

E_{Iconst} - set of totalities of values for criteria K_{Iconst};

E_{Ix} - set of totalities of values for criteria K_{Ix}.

The problem-solver can determine X_+ in two ways.

In the one technique he isolates, if possible, from the set E_I a subset $E_{I\hat{+}}$ $(E_{I\hat{+}} \sqsubset E_I)$ whose elements possess the following properties:

$$\forall \bar{e}_{I1} \varepsilon E_{I\hat{\ddagger}}, \ \forall \bar{e}_{Im} \varepsilon \ E_I \setminus E_{I\hat{\ddagger}}, (\bar{e}_{I1} \ \hat{P} \ \bar{e}_{Im} \vee \bar{e}_{I1} \ N \ \bar{e}_{Im}) \wedge$$

$$\wedge (\urcorner \ \exists \ \bar{e}_{In} \ \varepsilon \ E_{I\hat{\ddagger}} \ ; \forall \ \bar{e}_{ip} \ \varepsilon \ E_I \setminus E_{I\hat{\ddagger}} \ , \bar{e}_{In} \ N \ \bar{e}_{Ip})$$

Here $\hat{P} \sqsubset P$ is a binary relation which is interpreted as "clearly strictly more preferable than". Use of the term - "clearly" - presupposes that the relation of a clearly strict preference $\hat{P}$ between certain elements of the set E_I leads to a relation of a strict preference P between associated elements of the set E_Σ which have the same values in terms of the most important criterion set K_I no matter what the values are in terms of the remaining, less important criteria $K_\Sigma \setminus K_I$.

If $E_{I\hat{\ddagger}} \neq \emptyset$, then X_+ is determined, if this is possible. If $E_{I\hat{\ddagger}} \sqsubset E$, then to determine $E_{I\hat{\ddagger}}$ is to determine simultaneously X_+. X_+ is determined from the functional dependence on x in the case of $E_{I\hat{\ddagger}} \sqsubset E$ and from additional considerations in the case of $E_{I\hat{\ddagger}} \sqsubset E$.

If $X_+ = \emptyset$, the problem-solver can use the other technique.

He determines, if possible, the set of admissible controls X_I which influence estimated values for criteria of the set K_I. If the number of elements of the set X_I is low and fixed, then the problem-solver can determine the set $E_{I\star}$ of totalities of estimate values for the set K_I depending the set of controls $X_I(E_{I\star} \sqsubset E_I)$. If possible, he isolates from the set $E_{I\star}$ a subset $E_{I\star\hat{\ddagger}} \sqsubset E_{I\star}$. If $E_{I\star\hat{\ddagger}} \neq 0$, then the problem-solver determines the associated set $X_+ \sqsubset X_I$.

If, in using either approach,

$$E_{I\hat{\ddagger}} = \emptyset \vee E_{I\star\hat{\ddagger}} = \emptyset \vee X_+ = \emptyset$$

then to eliminate this situation the problem-solver returns to the beginning of the stage and changes either the most important set K_I or, if this does not remedy the situation, the set of criteria K_Σ associated with the chosen solution method.

Consequently, at each stage the problem-solver makes use of a limited amount of data and obtains a solution which can in general be regarded as a "particular" solution to the problem and should be updated or supplemented at subsequent stages.

The problem-solver discontinues the solution process if he feels that the set of "best" controls which he has obtained is satisfactory. Consequently, in compliance with the descriptive model of a problem-solver's behaviour the solution process is a multi-stage procedure, each stage consisting of many steps.

The flowchart for solving the problem at the i-th stage is shown in Fig. 3.

Let us briefly illustrate the separate elements of the flowchart using as an example a problem of selecting scientific manuscripts for publication.

At the first step the problem-solver determines the solution method which is supposed to be used at the first stage. Possible methods that might be considered are, for example, the use of information available for the problem-solver or the use of experts.

If the former is chosen in this case, the set K_Σ will consist of effectiveness criteria conditioned by the information circulating in the organization.

Further, the problem-solver determines in the set K_Σ the most important set of criteria K_I, which might be, for example, as follows:

$K_I = \ k_{I1}, k_{I2}, k_{I3}, k_{I4}\ .$

K_{I1} - availability of agreement with authors on preparing manuscript for publication by a certain deadline;
k_{I2} - significance of problems considered in manuscript;
k_{I3} - level of authors' professional skill;
k_{I4} - practical implementation of results obtained in manuscript.

For chosen criteria K_I the problem-solver determines the set E_I of totalities of values for criteria on appropriate scales, e.g. as follows:

for k_{I1}:
- agreement with authors is arranged;
- agreement with authors is not arranged.

for k_{I2}:
- there is every reason to achieve important results for national economy;
- probability of achieving important results is very high;

....

- probability of achieving important results is near zero.

for k_{I3}:
- authors gave great experience of scientific publication;
- authors have poor experience of scientific publication;

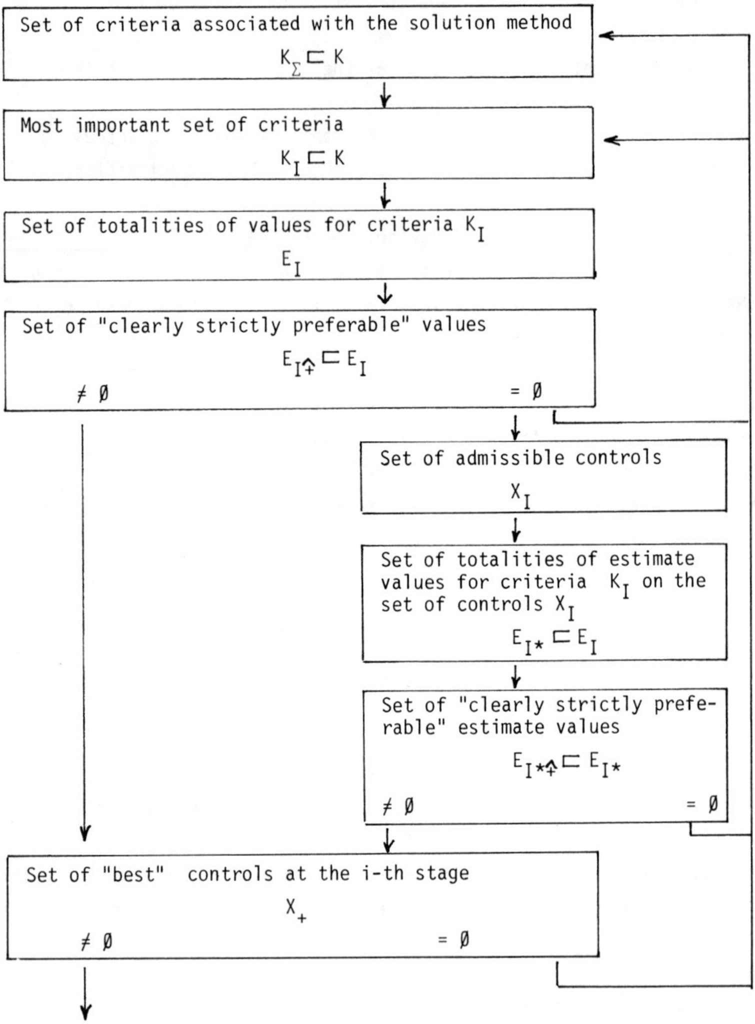

Fig. 3. Flowchart for the problem solution process at the i-th stage

- authors have no experience.

for k_{I4}:

- research is carried out simultaneously with practical implementation of results;
- results of research are expected to be implemented in next three years;
- the research is of a theoretical character.

At the next step the problem-solver determines from the set E_I a subset $E_{I\hat{+}}$ of "clearly strictly preferable" values, e.g. as follows:

- agreement with authors is arranged;
  (the value of the criterion k_{11})

or

- there is every reason to achieve important results for national economy;
  (the value of the criterion k_{12})

or

- authors have great experience in scientific publication and research is carried out simultaneously with practical implementation of results;
  (the values of criteria k_{I3}, k_{I4}).

On the basis of $E_{I\hat{+}}$ the problem-solver determines the "best" control X_+:

- the manuscripts having estimates which coincide with values of the set $E_{I\hat{+}}$ are selected for publication; remainder will be considered at nest stage.

It should be noted that in this particular case estimate values of manuscripts for criteria K_I are independent of x, i.e.

$$K_I \sqsubset K_{Iconst}, \quad E_{I\hat{+}} \sqsubset E_{Iconst}$$

The problem-solver then proceeds to the next stage.

Let us assume that the problem-solver dealing with the remaining manuscripts retains the solution method and the most important set of criteria unaltered. It is assumed that $E_{I\hat{+}} = \emptyset$ at this stage.

Since, as mentioned above, $K_I \sqsubset K_{Iconst}$, it follows that it is not necessary to determine the set of admissible controls X_I.

The problem-solver determines the set E_{I*} of totalities of estimate values of the remaining manuscripts for criteria K_I.

Let the n-th manuscripts have the following estimate values:
for k_{I1}: agreement with authors is not arranged;
for k_{I2}: probability of achieving important results is very high;
for k_{I3}: authors have poor experience of scientific publication;
for k_{I4}: research is carried out simultaneously with practical implementation of results.

Let us assume that the estimate values of other manuscripts except the n-th one are less preferable compared with those of the n-th manuscript.

The problem-solver considers estimate values of the n-th manuscript as "clearly strictly preferable" belonging to the set $E_{I*\hat{+}}$ and determines the "best" control X_+:
- the n-th manuscript is selected for publication and the remainder will be considered at the next stage.

The problem-solver then proceeds to the next stage.

The problem is considered to be solved if decisions "to publish or not to publish" have been adopted for each manuscript or if the problem-solver decides at a certain stage that further solution is unsuitable.

Descriptive models of the problem-solver's behaviour currently available [2,4,10,11] are used to develop interactive systems adaptable to the actual problem-solver's behaviour which help him to solve effectively complex ill-structured problems such as object ordering, resource allocation, planning and the training of managers.

CONCLUSIONS

The paper classifies problems to be solved in management systems and a widespread class of complex ill-structured problems is identified. A possible statement of such problems is given and descriptive models of the behaviour of experienced problem-solvers are shown to be useful in designing the solution procedure. The resultant solution procedure forms the core for interactive systems adaptable to the actual behaviour of problem-solvers.

Descriptive models of behaviour of experienced problem-solvers also permit:
- better analysis of the existing processes of problem solution, which are basic in management systems;

- an effective dialogue between researcher and problem-solver in a language comprehensible to the latter for a deeper insight into his behaviour;
- dissemination of know-how about highly skilled problem-solvers and training of less experienced problem-solvers;
- better introduction of normative models which are very difficult to interpret without knowledge of the actual problem solver's behaviour.

REFERENCES

1 Khaynish, S.V. - M. Blifernich — Problems of Decision Making in Organizational Systems (Survey). MTsNTI, Moscow, 1978.

2 Khaynish, S.V. - A.G. Vlasov — A Descriptive Approach to Modeling the Behaviour of a Decision Maker in Management Systems. - Problemy MSNTI, Moscow, MTsNTI, 1979, no. 1, p. 41-78.

3 Kozeletski, Yu. — Psychological theory of decisions, - State scientific edition, Warsaw, 1977,(in Polish).

4 Naylor, T.H. — Computer simulation experiments with models of economic systems. Wiley & Sons, Inc. N.Y. 1971.

5 March, J.G. - H.A. Simon — Organizations. John Wiley & Sons, New York, 1964.

6 — Normative and descriptive models for decision-making (Proceedings of the Soviet-American seminar). - Moscow, "Science", p. 168-175.

7 Roy, B. — Décisions avex critères multiples. Problêmes et methodes. "Metra International", 1972, 11, No. 1, p. 121-151.

8 Simon, H.A. — Information-processing theory of human problem solving. Handbook of learning and cognitive processes. Ed. by W.K. Estes, v. 5, Human information processing. 1978, p. 271-295.

9 Vlasov, A.G. - S.V. Khaynish — A Descriptive Approach to Modeling Human Behaviour in Solving a Resource Allocation

		Problem (Preprint) MNIIPU, Moscow, 1980.
10	Vlasov, A.G. - S.V. Khaynish	Simulating solution of ill-structured complex problems in management systems with the use of descriptive models. - Abstracts of Eighth Research Conference on Subjective Probability, Utility and Decision Making. Budapest, 24-28 August, 1981.
11	Yermakova, A.V. - S.V. Khaynish - L.N. Tsygankov	An algorithm for solution of a complex ill-structured management problem (with reference to planning information publications on geological surveying). Algorithms and programs / All-Union Research Institute of Mineral Raw Material Economics and Geological Surveying. Sectoral Fund of Algorithms and Programs "Geology". Issue 6(47) Moscow, 1981.

THEORY AND PRACTICE OF
MULTIPLE CRITERIA DECISION MAKING
C. Carlsson and Y. Kochetkov (editors)

SOME INPROVEMENTS TO THE REFERENCE POINT APPROACH FOR DYNAMIC MCLP

M. KALLIO, M. SOISMAA

Helsinki School of Economics
Runeberginkatu 14-16, 00100 Helsinki 10, Finland

ABSTRACT

This paper deals with two improvements to the reference point approach for trajectory optimization. First, a method to construct for each interactive iteration a feasible initial solution is presented. Its superiority with respect to CPU time to a straightforward approach of starting with a previous optimum basic solution is demonstrated with numerical experiments. Second, two approaches for smoothing optimal trajectories are presented. The first one employs adjustment via borrowing and saving, whereas the second one restricts the objective to a linear combination of predetermined smooth trajectories. Numerical experiments with these two approaches are also presented.

1. INTRODUCTION

Among the desired properties of interactive approaches to multiple criteria linear programming [3] are the following: (i) they must be applicable to the size of problems which appear in practice, (ii) they must have the ability to deal with a large number of objectives (in particular for handling trajectory objectives [5]), (iii) they must be easy to implement on a computer (given an LP code as a starting point), (iv) they must exhibit user-friendliness taking into account that decision-makers work at the terminal, and (v) they must provide satisfactory convergence in a reasonable number of interactive iterations (which does not necessarily mean convergence in a strict mathematical sense under an assumed utility function but convergence to a satisfying solution [5]).

This paper deals with the reference point approach of Wierzbicki [4] which directly satisfies properties (i) and (ii). Kallio et al [1] discuss a user-oriented approach to implementation which is only a minor modification to a standard LP code. They also provide a basic modification needed for convergence. The aim of this paper is to provide some improvements to user-friendliness and convergence.

After reviewing the reference point approach in Section 2 we present, in Section 3, a method for constructing a feasible initial solution for a new reference point. The purpose of this method is to decrease the user's waiting time for solutions of the interactive iterations. Results from numerical experiments are also presented. In Section 4 we deal with a problem of trajectory optimization. A general undesired property of dynamic LP is that the trajectories of various quantities tend to fluctuate. In particular this phenomenon may result in unsatisfactory objective trajectories when the reference point approach is applied. Interactive iterations resulting in such unacceptable trajectories are in fact useless and, if they are many, the method may fail. We present two approaches to accomplish smooth trajectories. Results from numerical experiments are also presented.

2. THE REFERENCE POINT APPROACH

We shall now briefly review the reference point approach for multicriteria linear programming (MCLP) as presented in Kallio et al [1]. Let A be in $\mathbb{R}^{m\times n}$, C in $\mathbb{R}^{p\times n}$, and b in $\mathbb{R}^m$ and consider a multicriteria linear program

(1) $Cx = q$

(2) $Ax = b$

(3) $x \geq 0$

where the decision problem is to determine a n-vector x of decision variables satisfying (2) and (3) and taking into account the p-vector q of objectives defined by (1). We assume that each component of q is desired to be as large as possible.

What we call a reference point or reference objective is a suggestion $\bar{q}$ by the decision-maker reflecting in some sense an aspiration level for the objectives. According to Wierzbicki [4], we consider for a reference point $\bar{q}$ a penalty scalarizing function $s(q-\bar{q})$ defined over the set of objective vectors q. Characterization of functions s, which result in Pareto optimum (or weakly Pareto optimum) minimizers of s over attainable points q is given by Wierzbicki.

If we regard the function $s(q-\bar{q})$ as the "distance" between the points q and $\bar{q}$, then, intuitively, the problem of finding such a minimum point means finding among the Pareto set the nearest point $\hat{q}$ to the reference point $\bar{q}$. However, as it will be clear later, our function s is not necessarily related to the usual notion of distance. Having this interpretation in mind, the use of reference point optimization may be viewed as a way of guiding a sequence $\{\hat{q}^k\}$ of Pareto points generated from the sequence $\{\bar{q}^k\}$ of reference objectives. These sequences will be generated in an interactive process and such interference should result in an interesting set of attainable points $\hat{q}^k$. If the sequence $\{\hat{q}^k\}$ converges, the limit point may be seen as a solution to the decision problem.

We shall apply a practical form of the penalty scalarizing function s(w), where minimization results in a linear programming formulation. We denote $w \equiv q - \bar{q}$, for brevity. Our function is given as follows:

(4) $s(w) = - \min \{\rho \min_i w_i , \Sigma w_i \} - \varepsilon w.$

Here ρ is an arbitrary penalty coefficient which is greater than or equal to p and $\varepsilon = (\varepsilon_1, \varepsilon_2, \ldots, \varepsilon_p)$ is a non-negative vector of parameters. If $\rho = p$, then (4) reduces to

(4') $s(w) = \rho \max_i - w_i - \varepsilon w;$

i.e. the minimum of s is attained according to the worst case criterion $\max - w_i$

corrected with a term $-\varepsilon\, w/p$ (which is small if ε_i is small for each i).

The reference point optimization problem when the scalarizing function (4) is applied is the following linear programming problem [1]:

find s_o, s, y, w, and x to

$$\text{minimize} \quad y - \varepsilon\, w \tag{5}$$

$$\text{subject to} \quad s_o - y - \gamma\, w = 0 \tag{6}$$

$$s - \gamma^T y - \rho\, w = 0 \, . \tag{7}$$

$$- w + Cx = \bar{q} \tag{8}$$

$$Ax = b \tag{9}$$

$$s_o,\ s \text{ and } x \text{ nonnegative.} \tag{10}$$

Here $\gamma = (1, 1, \ldots, 1)$ and $s = (s_1, s_2, \ldots, s_p)^T$ are p-vectors, and s_o and y are scalars. One may show [1] that if $\varepsilon > 0$ then the optimal solution $q = Cx$ is Pareto optimum.

3. A FEASIBLE INITIAL SOLUTION

Consider an interactive iteration. After the new reference point has been inserted, a natural idea for solving the resulting problem (5) - (10) is to start (the simplex method) with the optimal basis obtained from a preceding interactive iteration. (Now only the right-hand side has been changed.) The drawback to this approach is that this initial basis is usually infeasible. Therefore Phase I of the simplex method is needed, at the end of which the resulting feasible solution may be rather far from optimal. To avoid the difficulty caused by initial infeasibility, several approaches may be considered. First, if an (optimum) feasible basis is available for reference point $\bar{q}^1$, and if $\bar{q}^2$ is the reference point currently under consideration, then we may parametrize the reference point $\bar{q} = \bar{q}^1 + \Theta(\bar{q}^2 - \bar{q}^1)$, letting the parameter Θ increase from 0 to 1. Standard parametric programming starting with $\Theta = 0$ would be applicable to solve the problem for $\Theta = 1$ (i.e. for $\bar{q} = \bar{q}^2$). Tests (with a model mentioned below) with this approach, however, showed sometimes unsatisfactorily slow convergence (i.e. a very large number of basis changes were needed for parametrization). Second, the dual simplex method could have been applied for reoptimization, but software was not available. For these reasons an alternative approach was considered. In this case a previously obtained (optimum) feasible basic solution is employed to construct for the present problem a feasible (typically non-basic) solution and a related basis. Standard procedures are then applied to find a feasible basic solution and then Phase II of the simplex method is executed. We shall now describe how the initial solution can be constructed and thereafter we demonstrate the performance of this approach by numerical experiments.

3.1. Construction of an initial solution

Let us assume that we have an optimum basic solution $(s_0^*, s^*, y^*, w^*, x^*)$ for a reference point q^* of problem (5) - (10), and consider the new reference point $\bar{q}$.

Let $\bar{x} = x^* \geq 0$ so that $A\bar{x} = b$. Define $\bar{w}$ to satisfy (8) for $x = \bar{x}$ so that $\bar{w} = C\bar{x} - \bar{q}$. In order to satisfy the constraints (6) and (7), given $x = \bar{x}$ and $w = \bar{w}$, we define the values for $\bar{y}$, $\bar{s}_0$ and $\bar{s}$ as follows:

(11) $\quad \bar{y} = \max \{ - \sum \bar{w}_i, \max_i - \rho \bar{w}_i \},$

(12) $\quad \bar{s}_0 = \bar{y} + \gamma\bar{w} ,$

(13) $\quad \bar{s} = \gamma^T\bar{y} - \rho w.$

One may readily check that $\bar{s}_0 \geq$ and $\bar{s} \geq 0$. In summary, our construction has resulted in a solution $(\bar{s}_0, \bar{s}, \bar{y}, \bar{w}, \bar{x})$ which is feasible for problem (5) - (10) when the current reference point q is applied.

Obviously this solution may notbe a basic solution, and our next task is to define a related initial basis. This of course may be done in several ways. A natural choice is the basis which we obtained as the optimum for reference point q^*. If the variables y and w are in this basis (which is a condition easy to satisfy, because y and w are free variables), then the only non-basic variables at a non-zero level in the initial solution $(\bar{s}_0, \bar{s}, \bar{y}, \bar{w}, \bar{x})$ are among the slacks s_0 and s. Thus only the values of these non-basic slacks have to be set to start solution.

3.2 Numerical results

Because we are working interactively with the decision-maker at the terminal it is very important that runs are completed as fast as possible. The purpose of the numerical runs was to investigate the saving in computing time (and in the decision-maker's waiting time for a solution at each interactive iteration) when the above approach was applied and compared with the naive approach where an initial basic solution is employed.

The model used for tests is a dynamic linear programming model of a forest sector (i.e. a model of forestry and forest industries). There are approximately 700 variables and 550 rows in the 8-period model which has two trajectory objectives: industrial profit and forestry profit. To study the efficiency of our approach we performed experiments with five different reference points. These reference trajectories have been illustrated in Figure 1. An optimum basic solution corresponding to trajectory q* (of Figure 1) was employed to construct the initial feasible solution (and basis) for each of the five trajectories. The same basis was used to start the naive approach for comparison.

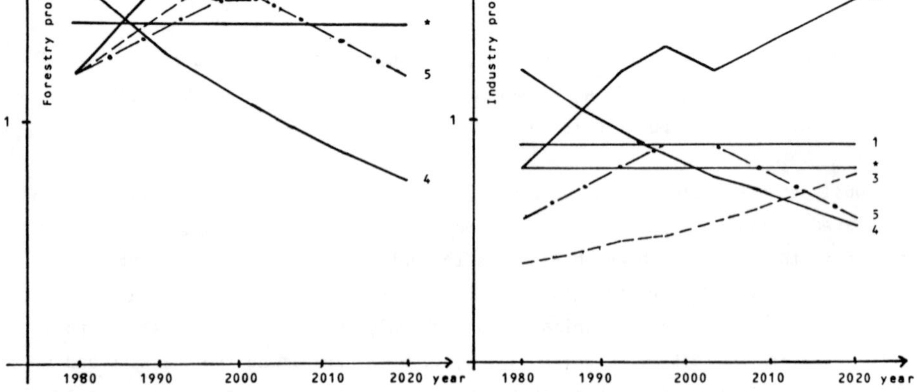

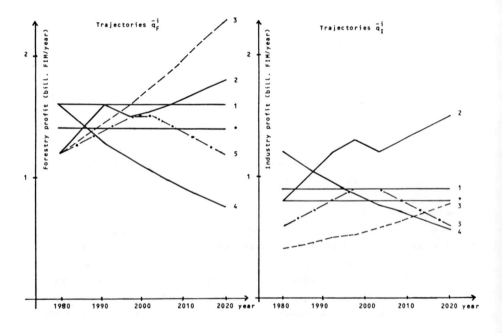

Fig. 1. Reference trajectories $\bar{q}^i = (\bar{q}_F^i, \bar{q}_I^i)$ used in experiments i = 1,2,3,4,5 and *.

Table 1 shows the results of the experiments. It reveals the total CPU time (on a VAX/780 computer when the MINOS code [2] was used) needed to find an optimum solution. Also the number of simplex iterations is indicated. The CPU time includes a problem set-up time which in each case (and for both approaches) was between 32 and 33 seconds.

Table 1. Solution time (in CPU-seconds) and the number of iterations for the naive approach (N) and the construction approach (C).

Reference trajectory	CPU seconds N	CPU seconds C	Iterations N	Iterations C
q^1	38	43	13	19
q^2	215	112	273	114
q^3	152	97	193	92
q^4	98	41	117	12
q^5	94	80	99	68
Total	597	373	695	405

We may conclude from Table 1 that the naive approach takes over 50 per cent more CPU time than does the approach described in Section 2.1. If we consider only the time required for iterations, then the naive approach more than doubles the required CPU time. In only one case (the first one) was the naive approach superior. In this case (due to similarities in the reference trajectories between q^* and $\bar{q}^1$) the initial basis was also feasible for the naive approach.

4. SMOOTHING THE TRAJECTORIES

Due to the properties of extreme point solutions, a drawback of dynamic LP is that the optimum trajectories tend to fluctuate over time. Because of the existence of multiple optima the trajectories can even be randomly placed. This does not appear desirable to a decision-maker who has chosen a reference point with smooth growth, for example. A standard way to avoid this problem is to restrict the derivatives of the trajectories. This may be done by setting bounds either on the relative or absolute change from one period to the next. If both lower and upper bounds are used, then for a T-period model 2T additional constraints (which are not of the type of simple upper bounds) are needed for each trajectory to be smoothed.

Another approach for smoothing is to restrict a trajectory to a linear combination of a finite number of predetermined smooth trajectories. Such linear combinations are supposedly smooth as well. The generating trajectories may be drawn individually for each application or some general approaches (e.g. the one presented in Section 4.1. below) may be used. The number of additional constraints needed for each trajectory is T; i.e. the increase is only one half compared with the alternative above. Furthermore, the loss in optimality (due to additional constraints imposed for smoothing) can be negligible, given that the number and shape of generating trajectories is properly chosen. On the other hand, bounds on derivatives may lead to an undesired loss in optimality when these bounds are tight enough to guarantee reasonable smoothness.

In the following we apply smoothing to the trajectories of objectives. First, we apply an approach which in fact does not restrict but relaxes the original problem. Second, we present one way of applying generating trajectories for smoothing. Finally, we discuss some numerical experiments with these approaches.

4.1 Adjustment approach

When the trajectory represents income (as is the case for forestry and for industry profit), an efficient approach for smoothing is to allow adjustment through saving and borrowing. We can thus save part of the profit from one period to the next one or vice versa. Accordingly, equation (8) becomes

(14) $- w + Cx + Dv = q$

Here the components of decision vector v refer to borrowing and investments over consequent periods. The matrix D transforms the effects of these activities into income trajectories simultaneously accounting for interest rates. If the borrowing and saving interest rates are assumed to be equal (as we do in experiments below), then a single non-sign-constrained component of v may represent both saving and borrowing. Otherwise, the interest rate for borrowing has to be greater than for saving (to avoid unboundedness), and separate non-negative components of v are needed for these two activities.

4.2 Generating approach

An alternative way of representing an objective trajectory as a linear combination of smooth generating trajectories is an expansion similar to the Fourier series.

If $q_k(t)$ is the kth (endogeneous) objective trajectory, we impose the following restriction for each t (t = 0, 1, ..., T-1) and k (suppressing k):

$$(15) \quad q(t) = d + \sum \{a_j \ \sin (jt\pi \ / \ 4\ (T-1)) + b_j \ \cos(jt\pi \ / \ 4\ (T-1))\}.$$

Here d, a_j and b_j (for each j) are free variables to be determined by the optimum solution, and T is the number of time periods in the model. Truncation of this expansion (which may be dependent on trajectory k) determines the number of generating trajectories, for each k. The larger this number is, the less restrictive is (15) and, on the other hand, the less smooth may the (optimum) trajectory $q_k(t)$ be.

4.3 Numerical experiments

The approaches given in Sections 4.1 and 4.2 were tested in six different cases for the forest sector model of eight periods. In the generating approach we used five different cases varying in the number of generating trajectories. Case i, for i = 1, 2, ..., 5, involves the first i terms (including the time-independent term d) of the expansion (15). We also present the original (non-smoothed) trajectories as well as the results from the experiments with the adjustment approach in Figure 2. Table 2 shows the loss of optimality resulting from the smoothing approach.

From these figures we may conclude that the original optimal trajectories are usually rather unsmooth with spikes. The trajectories from the adjustment approach behave ideally and (due to relaxation) they are superior to other trajectories. However, the generating approach yields variable results depending on the number of terms included in the truncation. The effects of the fluctuations in sin and cos terms become unsatisfactory when the number of terms becomes large. Such effects may be recognized in some of the Cases 4 and 5. Summarizing the results, three terms seem to be sufficient for the generating approach to smooth trajectories.

Table 2. The maximum deviations max - w_i for six runs and for three approaches: original non-smoothed, generating (case 3) and adjustment approach.

Run	Original	Generating approach	Adjustment approach
1	-400	-400	-903
2	-512	-512	-926
3	310	310	6
4	2060	2060	1256
5	296	304	52
6	1244	1244	751

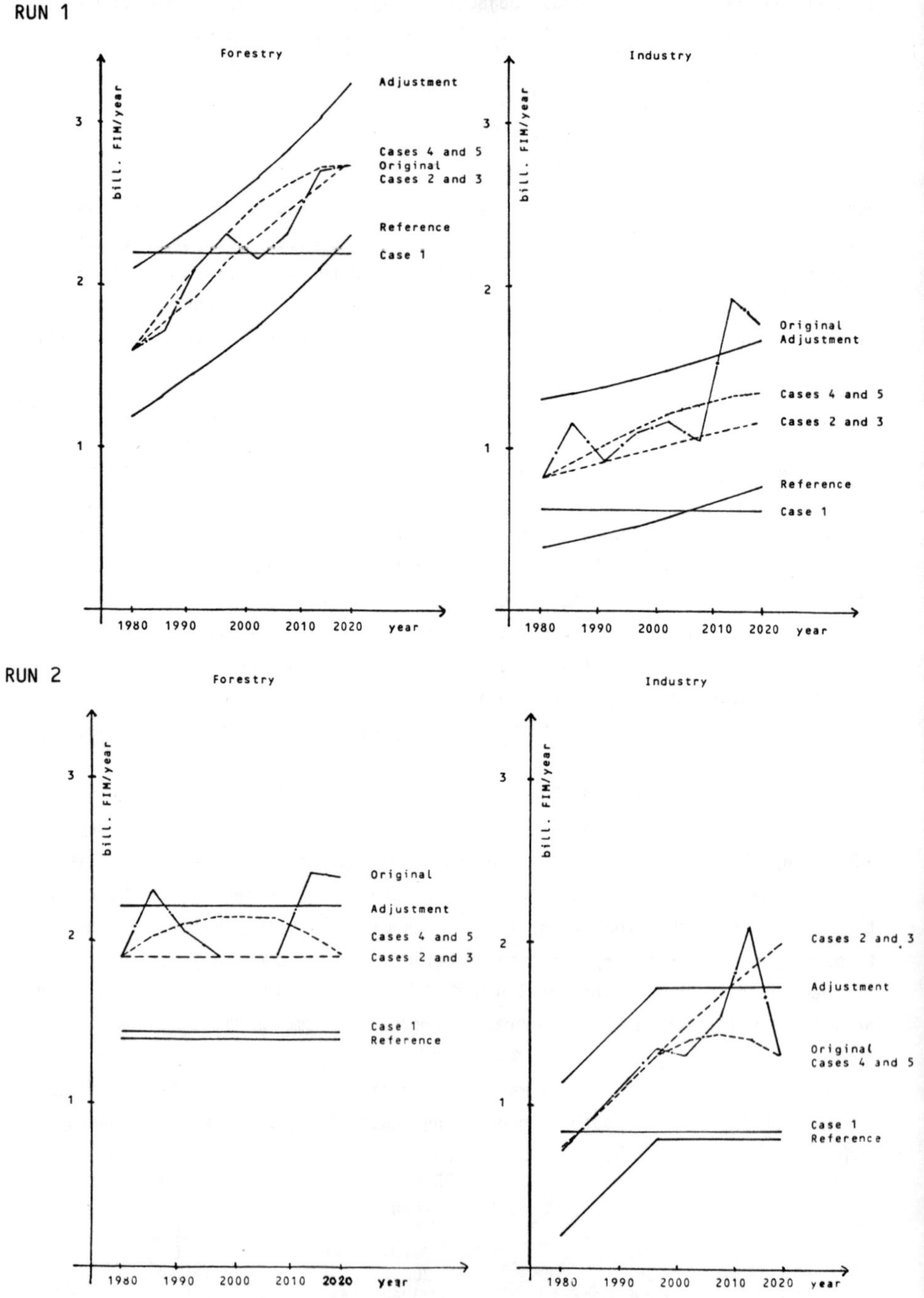

Figure 2. Trajectories of the adjustment approach and the generating approach (Cases 1,..., 5) compared to non-smoothed trajectories.

RUN 3

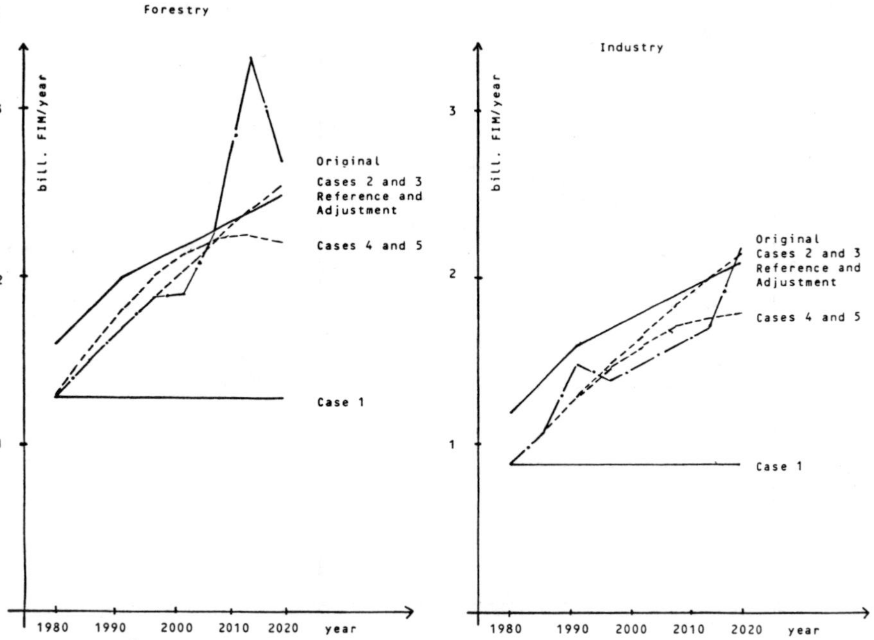
Forestry
bill. FIM/year
3
2
1
Original
Cases 2 and 3
Reference and
Adjustment
Cases 4 and 5
Case 1
1980 1990 2000 2010 2020 year
Industry
bill. FIM/year
3
2
1
Original
Cases 2 and 3
Reference and
Adjustment
Cases 4 and 5
Case 1
1980 1990 2000 2010 2020 year

RUN 4

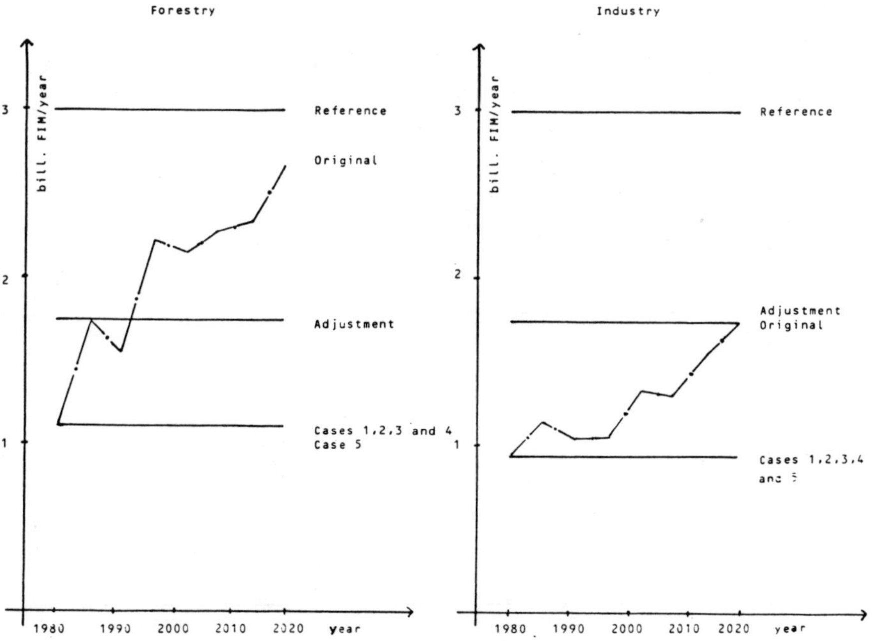
Forestry
bill. FIM/year
3
2
1
Reference
Original
Adjustment
Cases 1,2,3 and 4
Case 5
1980 1990 2000 2010 2020 year
Industry
bill. FIM/year
3
2
1
Reference
Adjustment
Original
Cases 1,2,3,4
1980 1990 2000 2010 2020 year

RUN 5

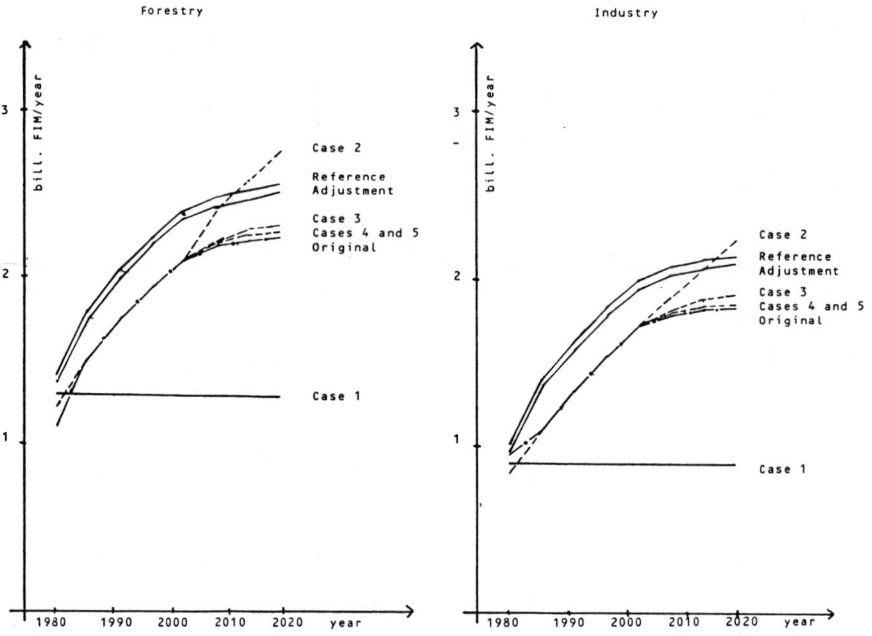
Forestry
Industry
bill. FIM/year
1
2
3
1980
1990
2000
2010
2020
year
Case 2
Reference
Adjustment
Case 3
Cases 4 and 5
Original
Case 1

RUN 6

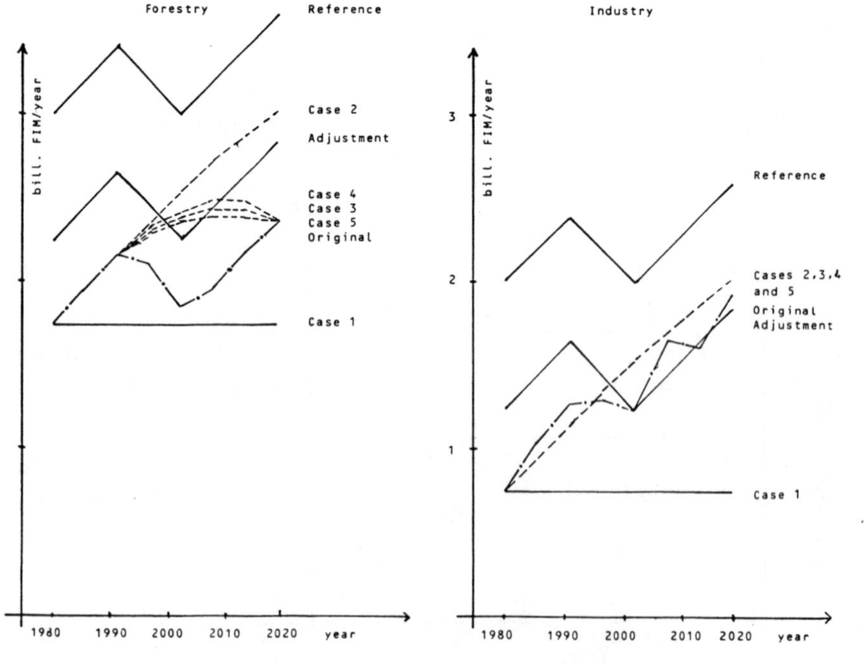
Forestry
Industry
bill. FIM/year
1
2
3
1980
1990
2000
2010
2020
year
Reference
Case 2
Adjustment
Case 4
Case 3
Case 5
Original
Case 1
Cases 2,3,4
and 5
Original
Adjustment

5. SUMMARY AND CONCLUSIONS

Related to the reference point approach (in particular, for trajectory optimization), we have explored two questions: (i) how to reduce the waiting time for a new Pareto optimum solution when the reference point is changed, and (ii) how to obtain smooth objective trajectories without significant loss in Pareto optimality.

Our approach for the first question is to employ Pareto solutions obtained in preceding iterations for constructing feasible initial solutions to the reference point optimization problem. Compared with a naive approach starting with a previous Pareto optimum basic solution considerable savings in computing time were obtained.

For smoothing we applied two approaches: one, where adjustment on trajectories is done via borrowing and saving, and another, where the objective is restricted to a linear combination of predetermined smooth trajectories. The latter approach is generally applicable, whereas the former one may be applied only when saving and borrowing have a meaningful real-life interpretation. Both approaches were successfully demonstrated with a number of numerical runs.

REFERENCES

1 Kallio, M., - A. Lewandowski - W. Orchard-Hays — An Implementation of the Reference Point Approach for Multiobjective Optimization. WP-80-35. Laxenburg, Austria: International Institute for Applied Systems Analysis, 1980.

2 Murtagh, B - M. Saunders — Large-Scale Linearly Constrained Optimization. Mathematical Programming 14 41-72, 1978.

3 Roy, B. - P. Vincke — Multicriteria Analysis: Survey and New Directions. European Journal of Operational Research 8 207-218.

4 Wierzbicki, A. — A Methodological Guide to Multiobjective Optimization. WP-79-122. Laxenburg, Austria: International Institute for Applied Systems Analysis, 1979.

5 Wierzbicki, A. A Mathematical Basis for Satisficing Decision Making. WP-80-90. Laxenburg, Austria: International Institute for Applied Systems Analysis, 1980.

THEORY AND PRACTICE OF
MULTIPLE CRITERIA DECISION MAKING
C. Carlsson and Y. Kochetkov (editors)

MULTIPLE-CRITERIA OPTIMIZATION UNDER UNCERTAINTY: CONCEPTS OF OPTIMALITY AND SUFFICIENT CONDITIONS

V.S. MOLOSTVOV

International Research Institute of Management Sciences
Schepkina Street 8, 129090 Moscow, USSR

ABSTRACT

The paper is concerned with control problems where
1. The system is controlled (managed) by n participants, the i-th participant wishing to "maximize" the value $I_i \in \mathbf{R}^{N_i}$ of his vector-valued objective function.

2. Each admissible control n-tuple $u=(u_1,\dots, u_n)$ is associated with sets $I_1(u) \subset R^{m_1},\dots, I_n(u) \subset R^{N_n}$ rather than with a single specific n-tuple of vectors $(I_1, \dots, I_n)$ in the system description. Any set of vectors $(I_1,\dots, I_n) \in I_1(u) x \dots x I_n x I_n(u)$ can occur with the use of a given u. Factors are discussed which are responsible for this multivalence of objective functions such as uncertainty of the mathematical description of the system, incompleteness of information, and the multi-level structure of the control process.

Proceeding from the generally accepted concepts of Pareto-optimality and maxmin solution the solution for a multicriteria optimization problem (n= 1) with feature 2 is defined. This concept leads to the concept of optimal solutions for a general case of $n \geq 2$; the saddle point (with $n = 2$, $I_2 = -I_1$) and the equilibrium point. Properties of these solutions are investigated. Methods are put forward for scalarization of the criteria (sufficient optimality conditions) which lead to the problem of maxmin for one or several monotone scalar functions.

In the problem of multi-criteria linear programming with uncertain coefficients of objective functions the optimal solutions are obtained by solving an extended (scalar) linear programming problem.

INTRODUCTION

This paper is concerned with optimization problems whose specifics include:

S1. The system is controlled by N participants whose interests do not coincide. The objectives of an individual participant in the control process cannot be expressed in terms of one index, which inevitably leads to the use of vectorial objective functions (criteria). The i-th participant is assumed to choose his admissible control $u_i \varepsilon U_i$ to obtain the highest possible value for each component I_i^j (j=1, ,,,, N_i) of his vectorial objective function I_i.

S2. For a number of reasons (see below) there is uncertainty in the outcome of control. When the participants choose their own admissible controls, the outcome (understood as values of vectorial objective functions) is determined in a multivalent way. Each n-tuple of admissible controls is associated in the mathematical model of the system, rather than with a specific n-tuple of vectors $I_1 \varepsilon R^{N_1}, \ldots, I_N \varepsilon R^{N_n}$, which are values of the criteria, with a certain n-tuple of set $I_1(u) \sqsubset \mathbb{R}^{N_1}, \ldots, I_n(u) \sqsubset \mathbb{R}^{N_n}$. In using the n-tuple of controls $u \varepsilon U_1 x \ldots x U_n$ any n-tuple of vectors $(I_1, \ldots, I_n) \varepsilon I_1(u) x \ldots x I_n(u)$ can occur.

These specifics are inherent in the control of most different systems such as industrial processes, economic planning, biological systems, etc. There are, however, three fairly general factors which lead to uncertainty in the outcome of control and, consequently, multivalence of objective functions.

(i) Uncertainty in mathematical description of the system to be controlled, incompleteness of a priori and current data on its state. Typically in control problems some system or exogenous signal parameters are known to vary only within specified ranges. In particular, the objective functions (indices of the control performance) are not necessarily known precisely. Thus, in a multiple criteria linear programming problem with objective functions $L_i(x)=c_i\ x$ (i=1,...,N) the only thing known about the coefficients $c_i \varepsilon \mathbb{R}^m$ is that they satisfy linear constraints, i.e. that the mN-vextor $c=(c_1, \ldots, c_N)$ belongs to some bounded polyhedron C. Then each admissible solution $x \varepsilon X$ is associated with a certain set $L(x)=\{L \varepsilon \mathbb{R}^N \mid L_i=c_i\ x, (c_1, \ldots, c_N) \varepsilon C\}$ of possible values of the objective function L. The sets L(x) are obviously bounded polyhedra in $\mathbb{R}^N$ with any x.

(ii) Multi-level structure of the game problem. In a two-level game an upper level player is the first to choose his control u , which he reports to lower level players. These then optimize their (possible vectorial) criteria by choosing controls $(v_1(u),\ldots, v_k(u))=v(u)$. The upper level player has to allow for the possibility that any control k-tuple $v \in V(u)$ from the set of optimum (e.g. Pareto-optimum) "responses" of lower level players can be realized. Therefore in optimizing a (possibly vectorial) criterion $I(u,v)$ by the upper level player each control u is associated with a set $I(u)=I(u,V(u))= \{I=I(u,v), v \in V(u)\}$ of possible values of the criterion I.

(iii) Specifics of the mathematical tools. Following N.N. Krasovskiĭ's mathematical formalization of positional strategies and the motions of the dynamic system so generated, each n-tuple of positional strategies of players is associated with a bundle of motions. Consequently, if the pay-off of each player is specified by a vector-valued function, this bundle of motions generates certain sets in associated spaces of player pay-off values.

The first specific feature (S1) results in multiple criteria game problems where each player wishes to optimize his own vectorial criterion (pay-off function). For this class of games refs [1, 2] report many findings where the equilibrium situation is defined (extending the well-known concepts of Pareto-optimality and Nash equilibrium) and the necessary optimality conditions are obtained. In refs [3, 4] these results were applied to antagonistic games with vector-valued pay-off functions, or games with two players of which one wishes to "maximize" and the other, to "minimize" the (same) vectorial function. In this case the concept of an equilibrium point [1, 2] is transformed into a definition of the saddle point of the vector-valued function [3, 4].

Recognition of uncertainty in the outcome of control (S2) results in game problems with multi-valued vectorial pay-off functions. This new class of problems remains little explored. References [5 - 8] investigated a particular case where for various static and dynamic systems a multi-valued vectorial objective function was optimized by one player or a coalition of all players who choose their controls in a coordinated way. The generally accepted concept of Pareto-optimality and the principle of the best guaranteed results [9] has led to some natural definitions of optimality [6] which become the concept of the Pareto optimum in the case of single-valued criteria. Reference [8] is concerned with a more general case where the original ordering in the space of vectorial criterion values is provided by an arbitrary convex acute cone (such as the positive orthant which is the case of Slater-optimality) rather than by a non-negative orthant as in Ref. [6]. The sufficient conditions obtained in [5 - 8] have been used in positional differential games [5, 7, 8] and difference-differential games [6].

The approach of [5 - 8] leads in this paper to a definition of the saddle point and a generalizing definition of the equilibrium point for game problems with multi-valued vectorial pay-off functions (if these are single-valued, these definitions practically coincide with the concept of a saddle point [3] and of the equilibrium point [2] .

Section 1 is introductory and discusses the specifics of the concept of optimality in the case of multi-valued pay-off functions. Section 2 gives definitions and sufficient conditions for saddle points (and Sect. 3, for equilibrium points) in the case of multi-valued pay-off functions of the players. An example of a multiple criteria linear programming problem with uncertain coefficients of objective functions is given for which a method of finding the optimal solution is described.

1. EXTREME POINTS OF MULTI-VALUED VECTORIAL FUNCTIONS

1.1 Multiple Criteria Optimization

Let us assume that on a set U of admissible controls a vectorial multi-valued pay-off function I(u) is determined with values in comp($\mathbf{R}^N$), or that each $u \in U$ is associated with a compact set $I(u) \sqsubset \mathbf{R}^N$ of feasible (if a given control u is chosen) values of the objective vector I. Assume that it is desirable to obtain the largest possible value of each component of the objective vector $I = (I^1,\dots,I^N)$. Consequently, we arrive at a multiple criteria optimization problem

$$\langle U, I(u), P\rangle \qquad (1.1)$$

where P is the non-negative orthant in $\mathbf{R}^N$. This problem has been investigated in [6]; in this article it is used as an auxiliary tool. Let us have a closer look at it.

In ref. [6] the notions of P1-, P2- and P3-optimalities were introduced; they spring to existence naturally because the vector function I(u) is multi-valued. The properties of associated optimum solutions have been studied. What follows is a formulation P2-optimality (to be hereafter referred to as P-extremality) different from but nonetheless equivalent to P2.

1.2. The Concept of an Extreme Point

Definition 1. A point $u^* \in U$ is referred to as the P-extreme point of the vectorial multi-valued function $I(u)$ on U iff

$$I(u) \not\subset I(u^*)+P_\emptyset \qquad \text{for all } u \in U. \tag{1.2}$$

Here $P_\emptyset = P\setminus\{0\}$ is the orthant P without zero; the sign $\not\subset$ means "does not contain", or that at least one point from $I(u)$ does not belong to the algebraic sum of sets in the right-hand side of the relation (1.2).

Consequently, with any $u \in U$, $u \neq u^*$, a vector $I'' \in I(u) \subset \mathbb{R}^N$ can occur which does not dominate (in the sense of ordering by means of P) any vector $I \in I(u^*)$. To put it differently, no matter how "poor" the result $I' \in I(u^*)$ is, in choosing $u \neq u^*$ a result $I'' \in I(u)$ can be obtained which at least along one coordinate is worse (smaller) than I' or, in the best case, $I''=I'$. Consequently, a deflection from u^* in the problem (1.1) cannot give a guaranteed improvement of the pay-off.

Some other properties of P-extremality were investigated in Ref. [6]. Thus it has been proved that if u^* is a solution of the maxmin problem

$$\max_{u\in U}\ \min_{I\in I(u)} E(I) = \min_{I\in I(u^*)} E(I) \tag{1.3}$$

for a continuous (scalar) function $E(I)$ which strictly increases for each variable, then u^* is P-extreme.

<u>Remark 1</u>. Definition 1 has no point if in the condition (1.2) $P_\emptyset$ is replaced by P. Indeed, with $u=u^*$ the conditon (1.2) does not hold.

At first glance, to define P-extreme points as u such that

$$\text{for any } u \in U \text{ or } I(u) + P \not\subset I(\bar{u}) + P \text{ or } I(u) + P = I(\bar{u}) + P \tag{1.4}$$

seems reasonable. This definition also coincides with that of Pareto-optimality if $I(u)$ is single-valued and with that of maxmin if N=1. Its significant disadvantage is that there are not sufficient conditions of the form (1.3) which hold for it. This is easily seen in the following

<u>Example</u>. $U=[0,1] \subset \mathbb{R}^1$, $N=2$, $I(u)=\{I=(I^1,I^2) \in \mathbb{R}^2 \mid (I^1+\frac{\sqrt{2}}{2}u)^2 + (I^2+\frac{\sqrt{2}}{2}u)^2 \leq (1-u)^2\}$

is the circle of radius $(1-u)$ with centre in $-\frac{\sqrt{2}}{2}(u,u)$ (see Fig.). With $E(I)=I^1+I^2$, we can see that all $u^* \in [0,1]$ meet the condition (1.3) and, consequently, are

P-extremal. But the condition (1.4) is not met with any $u^* \varepsilon [0,1]$.

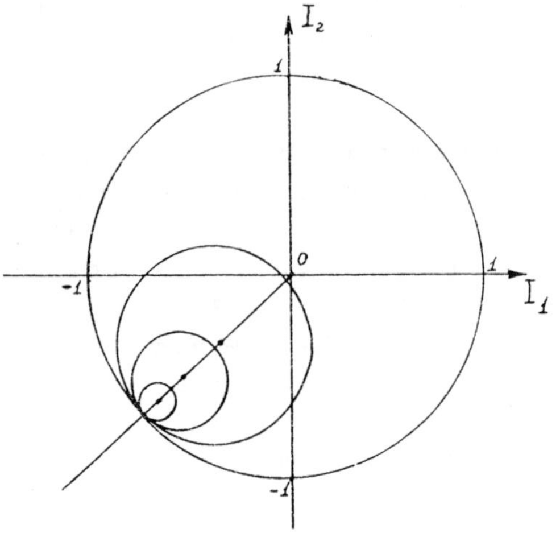

Fig. 1

Remark 2. The concept of P-extremality is further used in defining saddle and equilibrium points. Let us note that such constructions could be introduced by proceeding from the concepts of P1- or P3-extremality [6] and from the following definition of P4-extremality:

Definition 2. A point $u^* \varepsilon U$ is referred to as the P4-extreme point of the vectorial multi-valued function $I(u)$ iff

$$\overline{I(u)} \,\varepsilon\, \underline{I(u^*)} + P_{\emptyset} \qquad \text{for all } u \,\varepsilon\, U \tag{1.5}$$

where

$$\underline{I(u)}=(\min_{I\varepsilon I(u)} I^1,\ldots,\min_{I\varepsilon I(u)} I^N),\ \overline{I(u)}=(\max_{I\varepsilon I(u)} I^1,\ldots,\max_{I\varepsilon I(u)} I^N).$$

Since from the condition (1.5) follows the relation (1.2), P4-extreme points are also P-extreme.

Remark 3. Let U_{P1}, U_{P2}, U_{P3} and U_{P4} denote the associated sets of extreme points and U'_{P1} a subset of points $u \in U_{P1}$ such that $u' \neq u''$ implies $\underline{I(u')} \neq \underline{I(u'')}$. Then the following nestings take place

$$U'_{P1} \sqsubseteq U_{P2} \sqsubseteq U_{P3}\ , \quad U_{P4} \sqsubseteq U_{P1}\ . \tag{1.6}$$

By choosing various definitions of extremality it is possible to control the "breadth" of the set of optimum solutions to the problem (1.1).

2. SADDLE POINTS

2.1. P-Saddle Points

Let us consider an antagonistic game of two players with a multi-valued vectorial pay-off function

$$< U_1 \times U_2,\ I(u_1,\ u_2),\ P >. \tag{2.1}$$

Here u_1 and u_2 are strategies of the first and second players respectively and U_1 and U_2 are sets of their admissible strategies. Each pair $(u_1,\ u_2) \in U_1 \times U_2$ is associated with a set of possible values of the pay-off function $I(u_1,\ u_2) \in \text{comp}(\mathbf{R}^N)$; in other words, with the players choosing specific strategies u_1 and u_2, any vector $I \in I(u_1,\ u_2) \sqsubset \mathbf{R}^N$ can occur. The first wishes to obtain the largest and the second the least possible value of each component of vector $I=(I^1,\dots,I^N)$.

Definition 3. A pair of strategies $(u^*_1,\ u^*_2) \in U_1 \times U_2$ is referred to as the P-saddle point of the game (2.1) iff two conditions are met

$$I(u_1,\ u^*_2) \not\sqsubset I(u^*_1,\ u^*_2) + P_\emptyset \qquad \text{for all} \quad u_1 \in U_1, \tag{2.2}$$

$$I(u^*_1,\ u_2) \not\sqsubset I(u^*_1,\ u^*_2) - P_\emptyset \qquad \text{for all} \quad u_2 \in U_2. \tag{2.3}$$

In other words, $(u^*_1,\ u^*_2)$ is the P-saddle point of the game (2.1) iff the strategy u^*_1 is P-extreme in the multiple criteria optimization problem $< U_1, I(u_1, u^*_2), P) >$ and the strategy u^*_2 is (-P)-extreme in the multiple criteria optimization problem $< U_2,\ I(u^*_1,\ u_2),\ -P >$ . . .

In the particular case where the mapping $I:U_1 \times U_2 \to \mathbb{R}^N$ is single-valued, Definition 3 coincides with that of a K-saddle point from [3] if K=P. If also N = 1, we arrive at a conventional definition of the saddle point in an antagonistic two-person game.

Let us write $I' \underset{P}{\geq} I''$ if $I'-I'' \in P$, $I' \underset{P}{\gneq} I''$ if $I'-I'' \in P_\emptyset$ and $I' \underset{P}{>} I''$ if $I'-I'' \in \text{int}P$.

2.2 Sufficient Conditions for P-Saddle Points

Let scalar functions $E_1(I)$ and $E_2(I)$ be defined on $\mathbb{R}^N$, which are strictly monotone in the following sense:

$$I' \underset{P}{\gneq} I'' \text{ implies } E_i(I') > E_i(I'') \quad (i=1,\ 2). \tag{2.4}$$

Theorem 1. Let the continuous functions $E_1(I)$ and $E_2(I)$ be strictly monotone in the sense of (2.4) and for a pair of strategies $(u^*_1, u^*_2) \in U_1 \times U_2$ the equalities hold

$$\max_{u_1 \in U_1} \min_{I \in I(u_1, u_2^*)} E_1(I) = \min_{I \in I(u_1^*, u_2^*)} E_1(I), \tag{2.5}$$

$$\min_{u_2 \in U_2} \max_{I \in I(u_1^*, u_2)} E_2(I) = \max_{I \in I(u_1^*, u_2^*)} E_2(I).$$

Then (u_1^*, u_2^*) is the P-saddle point of the game (2.1).

The proof is not given because this Theorem is a corollary of Theorem 2 below.

Remark 4. It is sufficient to assume that the functions $E_1(I)$ and $E_2(I)$ be defined, continuous, and strictly monotone on the sets

$$I(U_1, u_2^*) = \bigsqcup_{u_1 \in U_1} I(u_1, u_2^*),\quad I(u_1^*, U_2) = \bigsqcup_{u_2 \in U_2} I(u_1^*, u_2) \qquad \text{respectively.}$$

3. EQUILIBRIUM POINTS

3.1 P-Equilibrium Points

Let us take up a non-cooperative game of n persons

$$< U_1 \times \ldots \times U_n, I_1, \ldots, I_n, P^1, \ldots, P^n \tag{3.1}$$

where u_i is the strategy of the i-th player which is chosen from the admissible set U_i, $u=(u_1,\ldots,u_n) \varepsilon U=U_1 \times \ldots \times U_n$; $I_i(u)$ is a multi-valued vectorial pay-off function of the i-th player, $I_i(u) \varepsilon \mathrm{comp}(\mathbb{R}^{N_i})$, P^i is a non-negative orthant in $\mathbb{R}^{N_i}$. The i-th player is assumed to wish to obtain as large value of each component of the vector $I_i=(I_i^1,\ldots,I_i^{N_i})$ as possible.

Let P_0^i denote the orthant P^i "without zero", $u_{n\setminus i}$ the (n-1)-tuple $(u_1,\ldots,u_{i-1}, u_{i+1},\ldots,u_n)$, and $(u^0_{n\setminus i},u_i)$ the n-tuple which results from u^0 by replacing u_i^0 by u_i.

<u>Definition 4</u>. A strategy n-tuple $u^0=(u_1^0,\ldots,u_n^0) \varepsilon U$ is referred to as <u>a P-equilibrium point for (3.1)</u> iff the following n conditions are met

$$I_i(u^0_{n\setminus i},u_i) \not\subset I_i(u^0) + P^i_\emptyset \quad \text{for all } u_i \varepsilon U_i \ (i=1,\ldots,n) \tag{3.2}$$

To put it differently, $(u_1^0,\ldots,u_n^0)$ is the P-equilibrium point of the game (3.1) iff for each i the strategy u_i is P-extreme in the multiple criteria optimization problem $< U_i, I_i(u^0_{n\setminus i},u_i), P^i >$. Consequently, the P-equilibrium point is stable in the following sense: if all the players but the i-th one choose the appropriate components of the equilibrium point as their strategies $u_j^0 (j\neq i)$, then the i-th player has no good reason either to deflect from "his own" component u_i^0 of the P-equilibrium point. Indeed, by virtue of (3.2) with any choice $u_i \neq u_i^0$ value $I_i'' \varepsilon I_i(u^0_{n\setminus i},u_i)$ can occur which does not dominate (in the sense of the relation $\geq_{p^i}$) any vector of the set $I_i(u^0)=I_i(u^0_{n\setminus i}, u_i^0)$.

In other words, no matter how poor the result $I_i' \varepsilon I_i(u^0_{n\setminus i}, u_i^0)$ is, by choosing $u_i \neq u_i^0$, a vector $I_i'' \varepsilon I_i(u^0_{n\setminus i},u_i)$ can be obtained which is worse (smaller) than I' along at least one coordinate or, in the best case, coincides with I'.

3.2 Properties of P-Equilibrium Points

1. If $n=2$, $P^1=-P^2=P$ and $I_1=-I_2=I$, then Definition 4 coincides with the above definition of a saddle point. If furthermore the function $I(u)$ is assumed to be single-valued ($I(u) \in \mathbb{R}^N$) what we have is a particular case of the saddle point of an non-cooperative game with a vectorial (single-valued) pay-off function (see Ref. [3]).

2. With single-valued $I_i(u)$ Definition 4 is essentially a particular case of definition of an equilibrium point [2]. If furthermore all $N_i=1$, then u^0 is a Nash equilibrium point [10].

3. Let all $N_i=1$, or $I_i(u) \sqsubset \mathbb{R}^1 (i=1,\ldots,n)$. Then P-equilibrium points in the game (3.2) coincide with Nash equilibrium points [10] in the game $\langle U_1 \times \ldots \times U_n, \min_{I_1 \in I_1(u)} I_1, \ldots, \min_{I_n \in I_n(u)} I_n \rangle$.

3.3 Sufficient Conditions for P-Equilibrium Points

Let scalar functions $E_i=E_i(I_i^1,\ldots,I_i^{N_i})$ be defined on $\mathbb{R}^{N_i}$ that are strictly monotone in the following sence

$$I_i' \underset{P^i}{\geq} I \qquad \text{implies} \quad E_i(I_i') > E_i(I_i'') \quad (i=1,\ldots,n). \tag{3.3}$$

Theorem 2. Let the continuous functions $E_i(I_i)$ $(i=1,\ldots, n)$ satisfy the conditions of strict monotonicity (3.3) and for a strategy n-tuple $u^0=(u_1^0,\ldots,u_n^0) \in U$ n equalities hold

$$\max_{u_i \in U_i} \min_{I_i \in I_i(u^0_{n\smallsetminus i},u_i)} E_i(I_i) = \min_{I_i \in I_i(u^0_{n\smallsetminus i},u_i^0)} E_i(I_i) \qquad (i=1,\ldots n). \tag{3.4}$$

Then u^0 is a P-equilibrium point.

Let us prove by contradiction. Let u^0 satisfy the conditions (3.4) but not to be a P-equilibrium point. Then for at least one i there exists a strategy $\tilde{u}_i \in U_i$ such that

$$I_i(u^0_{n\smallsetminus i},\tilde{u}_i) \sqsubset I_i(u^0) + P^i_\emptyset \tag{3.5}$$

or for any $\tilde{I}_i \in I_i(u_{n\smallsetminus i},\tilde{u}_i)$ there is $I_i \in I_i(u^0)$ such that $\tilde{I}_i \underset{P^i}{\geq} I_i$.

Let $I_i' \in \text{Arg} \min_{I_i \in I_i(u^o_{n \smallsetminus i}, \tilde{u}_i)} E_i(I_i)$. Since $I_i' \in I_i(u^o_{n \smallsetminus i}, \tilde{u}_i)$ for a certain $I_i^o \in I_i(u^o) = I_i(u^o_{n \smallsetminus i}, u^o_i)$, we have a relation $I_i' \underset{p^i}{\geq} I_i^o$ from which, with due regard for (3.3), we have

$$\min_{I_i \in I_i(u^o_{n \smallsetminus i}, \tilde{u}_i)} E_i(I_i) = E_i(I'_i) > E_i(I_i^o). \tag{3.6}$$

On the other hand, from the condition (3.4) we have

$$E_i(I_i^o) \geq \min_{I_i \in I_i(u^o_{n \smallsetminus i}, u^o_i)} E_i(I_i) = \max_{u_i \in U_i} \min_{I_i \in I_i(u^o_{n \smallsetminus i}, u_i)} E_i(I_i). \tag{3.7}$$

Combining (3.6) and (3.7) we have an inequality

$$\min_{I_i \in I_i(u^o_{n \smallsetminus i}, \tilde{u}_i)} E_i(I_i) > \max_{u_i \in U_i} \min_{I_i \in I_i(u^o_{n \smallsetminus i}, u_i)} E_i(I_i) \tag{3.8}$$

which can be written in the form

$$\Phi(u_i) > \max_{u_i \in U_i} \Phi(u_i) \qquad (\tilde{u}_i \in U_i) \tag{3.9}$$

where $\Phi(u_i)$ denotes the function to be maximized in (3.8).

Inconsistency of the relation (3.9) proves the Theorem.

Remark 5. Validity of Theorem 2 follows also from the fact that from the conditions (3.4) and the results of ref. [6] (Theorem 2.1) it follows that the strategy u_i^o is P-extreme in the multiple criteria optimization problem

$$\langle U_i, I_i(u^o_{n \smallsetminus i}, u_i), P^i \rangle \qquad (i=1,\ldots,n).$$

Remark 6. It is sufficient to assume that the function be defined, rather than on the entire space $\mathbb{R}^{N_i}$, only on the set

$$I_i(u^o_{n \smallsetminus i}, U_i) = \bigsqcup_{u_i \in U_i} I_i(u^o_{n \smallsetminus i}, u_i) \qquad (i=1,\ldots,n).$$

Corollary. If there are constant vectors $\alpha_i \in \mathbb{R}^{N_i}$, $\alpha_i \underset{p^i}{>} 0$ $(i=1,\ldots,n)$ such that

$$\min_{I_i \in I_i(u^o_{n\setminus i}, u^o_i)} \sum_{1\le k\le N_i} \alpha^k_i I^k_i = \max_{u_i \in U_i} \min_{I_i \in I_i(u^o_{n\setminus i}, u_i)} \sum_{1\le k\le N_i} \alpha^k_i I^k_i , \qquad (3.10)$$

then u^o is a P-equilibrium point.

Indeed, it is easily seen that the functions $E_i(I_i) = \sum_{1\le k\le N_i} \alpha^k_i I^k_i$ meet the monotonicity condition.

Solutions of the equation set (3.10) make $(\sum_{1\le i\le n} (N_i-1))$ parametric family of equilibrium points (one can assume that $\sum_{1\le k\le N_i} \alpha^k_i = 1$).

3.4 Some Possible Extensions

Let us note that the above concepts and findings for P-extreme, P-saddle and P-equilibrium points permit an extension to a more general case where the preference relations of the players are given by arbitrary convex acute cones Λ^i in the spaces $\mathbb{R}^{N_i}$. To do this, in Definitions 1, 3, and 4 and in formulations of Theorem 1 and 2 P^i is replaced by Λ^i.

For extreme points this extension is actually provided in ref. [8]. Furthermore, a case can be considered when the pay-off functions take on values in real Banach spaces that are ordered by using convex acute cones.

4. EXAMPLE. A MULTIPLE CRITERIA LINEAR PROGRAMMING PROBLEM

Let us assume that N linear functions $L^i(x)=c_i x=\sum_{1\le k\le m} c^k_i x^k$ are defined on the polyhedron $X\subset\mathbb{R}^m$. Accurate values of coefficients $(c^1_i, \dots , c^m_i)=c_i$ of these objective functions are not specified but the vector $c=(c_1,\dots,c_N)$ is known to belong to a specified bounded polyhedron in the space $\mathbb{R}^{mN}$: $c \in C \subset \mathbb{R}^{mN}$. To put it differently, linear constraints for these coefficients are specified. Since a linear transformation of the polyhedron is also a polyhedron the set $L(x)= \{ L\in \mathbb{R}^N \mid L^i=c_i x, (c_1,\dots,c_N)\in C \}$ of all values of the vectorial objective funcion L possible with choice of a given $x \in X$ is a bounded polyhedron in $\mathbb{R}^N$.

Assume that by choosing $x \in X$ it is desirable to obtain the largest possible value of each coordinate of the objective vector $L=(L^1,\dots,L^N)$, or that the following multiple criteria optimization problem should be solved (see (1.1))

$$< X, L(x), P > \tag{4.1}$$

It is helpful to regard a set of P-extreme points as a solution of this problem: analogously, in the case of a single-valued objective vector the set of Pareto-optimum points is regarded as the solution.

The sufficient conditions of P-extremality (1.3) take, in this problem, the form

$$\max_{x\in X} \min_{L\in L(x)} E(L) = \min_{L\in L(x^*)} E(L) . \tag{4.2}$$

Let the scalarization function be a linear function $E\alpha(L) = \sum_{1\leq i\leq N} \alpha^i L^i = L$ with weighting coefficients $\alpha^i>0$ $(i=1,\dots,N)$. Then the condition (4.2) can be rearranged into

$$\max_{x\in X} \min_{c\in C} \sum_{1\leq i\leq N} \alpha^i c_i \; x = \min_{c\in C} \sum_{1\leq i\leq N} \alpha^i c_i \; x^* \tag{4.3}$$

We have thus arrived at a problem of maxmin for the bilinear function $E\alpha(L) = \sum_{1\leq i\leq N} \alpha^i c_i \; x$ on the polyhedra X and C. This problem has been fairly well explored . If the set of vertices $\{c^{(s)} = (c_1^{(s)},\dots, c_N^{(s)}),\ s=1,\dots,S\}$ of the polyhedron C is known, it is possible to make use of the fact that the minimum in (4.3) is obtained on one of the vertices $c^{(s)}$ and represent the sufficient conditions (4.3) in the form

$$\max_{x\in X} \min_{1\leq s\leq S} \sum_{1\leq i\leq N} \alpha^i c_i^{(s)} \; x = \min_{1\leq s\leq S} \sum_{1\leq i\leq N} \alpha^i c_i^{(s)} \tag{4.4}$$

This problem is in turn equivalent to a linear programming problem

$$y \to \max_{x\in X} \tag{4.5}$$

under additional conditions

$$y \leq \sum_{1\leq i\leq N} \alpha^i c_i^{(s)} x \qquad (s=1,\dots, S). \tag{4.6}$$

If there are too many vertices of the polyhedron C and the dimension of the problem (4.5) - (4.6) is too high, then direct methods of solving the maxmin problem (4.4) are more helpful. The function $\Psi(x)=\min\limits_{1\leq s\leq S}\sum\limits_{1\leq i\leq N}\alpha^i c_i^{(s)} x$ is a continuous piecewise linear concave function. Therefore to find approximately its maximum point x* (this point is the desired P-extreme solution of the problem (4.1)) iterative methods of non-smooth optimizations are helpful, in particular those where a generalized gradient is used [11] .

REFERENCES

1 Kurzhanskiĭ A.B. - M.I.Gusev On multicriteria solutions in game-theoretic problems of control. Proc. IIASA Workshop on Decision Making with Multiple Conflicting Objectives, Vol. 2, Laxenburg, 1975, 51-67.

2 Gusev, M.I. - A.B. Kurzhanskiĭ On Equilibrium Points in Multiple Criteria Game Problems. Doklady AN SSSR, Vol. 229, No. 6, 1976.

3 Varga, Z. On Saddle Points of Vectorial Functions. In: Existence of Solutions, Stability and Availability of Information in Game Theory, Kalinin University Press, 1979, 3-19.

4 Varga, Z. On a Cooperative Pursuit - Evasion Game. Vestnik Moskovskogo Universiteta. Seriya "Vychislitelnaya matematika i Kibernetika", No, 1, 1979.

5 Zhukovskiĭ, V.I., - V.S. Molostvov Pareto-Optimality of Positional Controls. Abstracts of Papers at the All-Union Conference on Dynamic Control, Sverdlovsk, 1979, 99-101).

6 Zhukovskiĭ, V.I. - V.S. Molostvov On Pareto-Optimality in Cooperative Differential Games with Multi-Valued Objective Functionals. In: "Mathematical Methods in Systems Theory", All-Union Institute for Systems Studies, Moscow, 1980, 96-108.

7 Molostvov, V.S. On Slater Optimality in A Class of Games. Abstracts of 9th IFIP Conference on Optimization Techniques. Warsaw, 1979, 163.

8 Molostvov, V.S. - V.I. Zhukovskiĭ — On Λ -Optimality in a Class of Cooperative Many Player Differential Games. Lecture Notes in Control and Information Sciences. Vol. 22: Optimization Techniques. Proceedings of the 9th IFIP Conf. on Optimiz. Techniques, Warsaw. 1979, Part 1, 489-498. Springer Verlag, 1980.

9 Germeyer, Yu.B. — Introduction into Operations Reserach. Nauka. Moscow, 1971.

10 Nash, J. — Non-Cooperative Games. "Ann.Math.", Vol. 54, No. 2, 1961, 286-195.

11 Shor, N.Z. — Methods for Minimization of Nondifferentiable Functions and Their Applications. Naukova dumka. Kiev. 1979.

THEORY AND PRACTICE OF
MULTIPLE CRITERIA DECISION MAKING
C. Carlsson and Y. Kochetkov (editors)

SIMS, AN INTERACTIVE MULTI-CRITERIA SEARCH SYSTEM

O.A. SHESTAKOV

International Research Institute of Management Sciences
129090, Moscow, Schepkina str., 8

ABSTRACT

The paper discusses those multi-criteria search problems in which objects of choice are characterized in terms of two sets of indices: parameters and criteria. The problem is to find a combination of parameter values which will ensure the most preferable, from the decision-maker's point of view, combination of criterion values. An interactive system for solving such problems is described. The aim in developing the system was to give users who have no special knowledge and experience of formalized methods of decision-making a software tool for solving the multi-criteria search problems they face in their professional activity.

1. INTRODUCTION

We shall discuss those multi-criteria search problems in which objects of choice are characterized in terms of two sets of indices: parameters and criteria. Parameters, which are controlled variables, describe the technological or design features of objects of choice and the performance criteria are their operational output characteristics. For each parameter vector the vector of criterion values can be computed or measured. What is required is to find a combination of parameter values which will insure the most preferable, from in the decision-maker's point of view, combination of criterion values.

Problems of multi-criteria search arise in widely different fields of human activity. What follows are several examples.

1. The mechanism to be designed is characterized in terms of design parameters and a set of performance criteria. In the parameter space a region of admissible values is specified. The criterion values for specified values of the parameters are obtained by computing a mathematical model. Parameter values must be found for which the most preferable combination of values for performance criteria is obtained [1].

2. The manufacture of a new material is described by a set of process parameters such as temperature and pressure. The quality of the material is described in terms of a set of criteria each of which depends on the values of the process parameters. Parameter values have to be found wich result in the most preferable combination of qualities. In this problem the values for criteria can be either computed or measured directly.

3. Many chemical products such as fuels, oils, and paints are obtained by blending. The product properties vary with the concentration of the components. The objective is to find concentrations giving the most preferable combination of product properties (quality criteria).

In many cases the set of alternatives is specified implicitly; computation or measurement yields only isolated vectors for criterion values which are associated with chosen parameter values. This prevents the direct application of conventional approaches to solving multi-criteria problems [2-4]; therefore special methods and procedures have to be developed.

Another specific feature of such problems is the existence of several local optimal for preferences on the set of admissible parameter values (i.e. there are points a^{+i} in the parameter space each of which gives the most preferable combination of criterion values among all admissible points in a certain neighborhood of a^{+i}).

In a general case solution of this kind of problem proceeds through several stages [5]:

- design of a mathematical model to describe the dependence of the criteria on the parameter values;
- building up a network E_a of points which are uniformly distributed on the set of admissible parameter values D_a and computation of criterion vectors which are associated with these points;
- preselection of points in the network E_a and the associated vectors E_X. At this stabe such operations can be used as separation of the Pareto subset E_X^P from the set E_X; rejection of versions which do not satisfy the constraints on criterion values, etc.;
- choosing initial points in the Pareto subset E_X^P from which to search for the most preferable alternatives;
- search for the most preferable alternatives.

In solving specific problems some stages can be omitted. Thus in the case of a finite set of versions there is no need to construct a network E_a.

Specific statements of multi-criteria search problems can differ significantly in the form of:

- the set of objects (discrete or continual);
- constraints on parameter and criterion values;
- the mapping by which the parameter values and criterion values are linked and in the way of obtaining the mapping (computation or measurement).

Also, depending on the opportunity of decison-makers, information about preferences can be received in different forms such as

- quantitative estimates;
- interval estimates;
- ranking by preference.

Consequently, each real-life problem has to be solved by using specific methods and procedures. An expert in the particular kind of problem is needed each time.

2. SIMS, A MULTI-CRITERIA SEARCH SYSTEM

The goal of developing SIMS is to give users who have no special knowledge and experience of formalized methods of decision-making a software tool for solving the multi-criteria search problems they face in their professional activity.

The aim in developing the system was to design in advance schemes and algorithms for different statements of the problem and to program them so that, in response to the user's information about the specifics of his problem, the software would provide the necessary scheme and algorithms for a solution of the problem.

SIMS is implementable in PDP 11/70 computers and includes three levels of sub-routines.

(1) The identifying sub-routine, which displays questions on problem statements and, depending on responses from the user, chooses the control sub-routine needed to implement the appropriate solution procedure. If the user's program is beyond the system's capabilities, the sub-routine tells him so.

(2) Control sub-routines, which implement solution procedures by calling up the appropriate working sub-routines. Depending on the user's answers as to the most appropriate format of data on preferences (point-wise estimates, interval estimates, ranking, etc.), the sub-routine chooses the method of search for the most preferable alternatives.

The first version of the system now implements four solution procedures, each having three versions depending on the information about preferences received from the decision-maker.

(3) Working sub-routines, which implement specific methods and procedures to be used in solving the problem. These include:

- a check of constraints on parameter values;
- computing the criterion values from specified values for the parameters;
- plotting a sequence of uniformly distributed points;

- separation of Pareto set points from the specified set;
- choice of points which meet constraints on values for the criteria;
- a search for the most preferable alternatives on the basis of data about preferences in the form of point-wise estimates for compensating increments;
- a search for the most preferable alternatives on the basis of the ranked increments.

Some auxilary sub-routines also belong to this category.

SIMS can be expanded by increasing the number of control and working sub-routines to cope with the problems it is capable of tackling.

3. SOLVING THE PROBLEM OF MULTI-CRITERIA SEARCH IN THE PRESENCE OF THRESHOLD-LIKE CONSTRAINTS ON VALUES OF THE CRITERIA

This section will describe a solution procedure when the set of problem versions is continual, the criteria have threshold values, and the information about preferences is given as a ranking of criterion value increments.

First let us explain the concept of threshold values.

In conventional approaches to the solution of choice problems where the criteria are objectively measurable continuous numerical values, the preferences of decision makers are assumed to be continuous; in other words, it is assumed that small changes in criterion values result in small changes in the usefulness of the object chosen. In many real problems, however, the dependence of usefulness on the criterion and/or parameter values is not necessarily smooth. Some criteria and/or parameters may have certain critical threshold values; if these are exceeded, the usefulness changes abruptly. Thus, if a choice has to be made between the options of a project whose deadline is fixed, then the deadline is the threshold; if this is exceeded, the usefulness of the option is significantly reduced.

There are at least three groups of situations in which threshold values for criteria may occur.

1. The presence of resource, technological, or normative/plans, rules, etc./ constraints which can be broken only at the expense of additional cost, effort, etc.

2. Presence of such criterion values, exceeding which plans the objects in another quality category (product grade, class of instruments, etc.).

3. Situations where the object should excel certain prototypes. For example, a new product to be manufactured and compete with old ones. In this case the characteristics of the prototypes may play the role of threshold values for the new object.

Other situations which give rise to threshold values are also conceivable.

Now let us consider some preference features if there are threshold values for the criteria. This is necessary for an understanding of the solution procedure.

Let the objects of choice be project versions which are characterized in terms of two criteria: S, the project cost, and T, the time of its implementation, and let planned values of these indices, S^o and T^o, be given. Let us also assume that the decision-maker wishes to reduce both the cost and time. The set of project versions, which is represented as the plane ST, is divided by $S = S^o$ and $T = T^o$ lines into four regions to be referred to hereafter as orthants:

$A_I = \{ S, T \mid S \leq S^o, T \leq T^o \}$ is the orthant where the constraints on cost and time are met;

$A_2 = \{ S, T \mid S \leq S^o, T > T^o \}$

$A_3 = \{ S, T \mid S > S^o, T \leq T^o \}$

- are the orthants where one of the constraints is broken;

$A_4 = \{ S, T \mid S > S^o, T > T^o \}$ is the orthant where both constraints are broken.

Within each orthant small increments in the criteria are associated with small changes in the alternative usefulness, whereas going over from one orthant to another entails an abrupt change in usefulness because breaking the constraints specified by the plan significantly reduces the usefulness of an object. If the decision-maker's system of preferences is represented by a utility function U(S, T), then its plot has the form shown in Fig. 1.

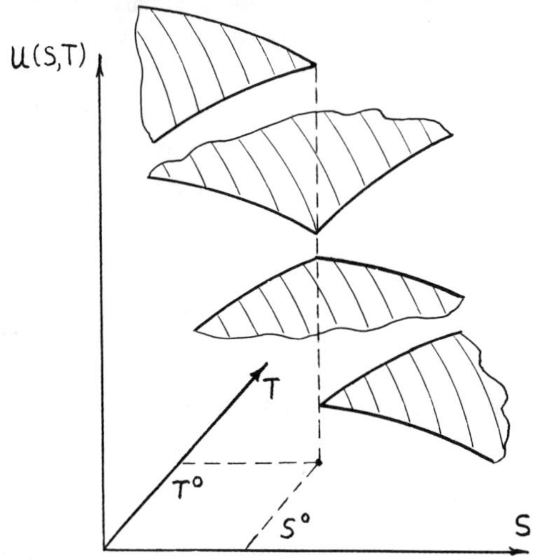

Fig. 1 The plot of the utility function

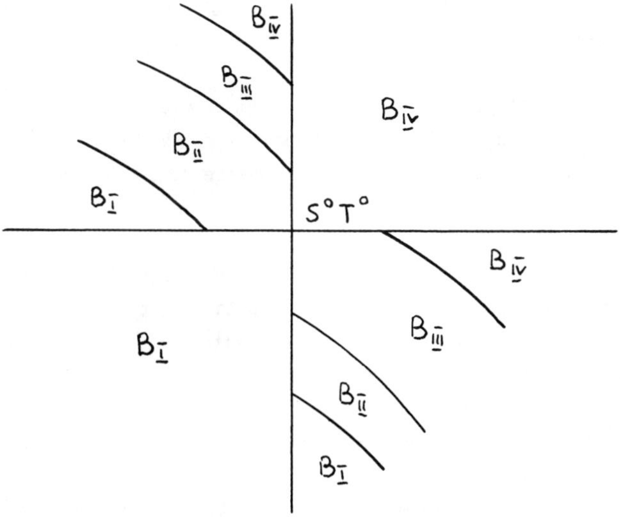

Fig. 2 Indifference curves and dominance zones

The plot of the function U(S, T) consists of four continuous pieces over the orthants A_i, i =[1, 4]and spaced along the value axis.

Figure 2 shows level curves of the utility function U(S, T) (indifference curves) on the plane S, T. The solid lines show those indifference curves which, together with the straight lines $S = S^o$ and $T = T^o$, form the boundaries of four domination zones, B_I, B_{II}, B_{III} and B_{IV} such that for any $x \in B_i$ and $y \in B_j$, $i > j$, it is true that $x \succ y$ where $\succ$ is the strict preference relation.

In Figs 1 and 2 it is seen that whether points in the vicinity of the point S^o, T^o belong to any of the four domination zones depends exclusively on whether these points belong to one of the orthants. The larger the changes in usefulness on the boundaries $S = S^o$ and $T = T^o$, the larger the vicinity where this is true.

Another important point is that a drop in usefulness due to breaking the constraints in terms of one of the criteria may be offset by a significant reduction in the value of another criterion.

Now let us take a multi-criteria search problem where the aim is to find an alternative a^+, $x^+ \in D$ which best accords with the decision-maker's preferences concerning the set of admissible alternatives.

Let us assume that the decision-maker's system of preferences includes threshold values and is monotone (the latter implies that for values of each of the criteria the rule "the more the better" or the inverse rule "the less the better" is true).

At first glance the simplest approach to solving this problem is to find the most preferable version in each non-empty (i.e. containing points of the set D) orthant and then to find the most preferable alternative among them. Implementation of this approch, which involves examining all the orthants, requires that the decison-maker provide a large amount of information, which significantly reduces the likelihood of its application.

The approach embodied in SIMS makes use of the features of the preferences in problems where the criteria have threshold values. First, the most preferable alternative is found in a non-empty orthant of the higher rank; then, using this orthant as the reference, more preferable alternatives are sought in other orthants by using fairly simple estimates. This approach reduces the amount of expert information required and also reduces most of the solution procedure to purely computer operations.

The interactive solving procedure is a sequence of stages some of which are tackled by the computer without the decision-maker taking part (denoted below as C); some by the decision-maker (denoted as M): and some through interaction of man and computer (denoted as MC). As detailed description of the procedure would take much space, certain unimportant detailes are omitted in the description which follows.

1st stage (C). The set of admissible vectors for parameters D_a is covered by a network E_a of uniformly distributed points. Sobol's sequence [6] is used to construct this network.

2nd stage (C). For each point of the network E_a criteria values are computed; as a result, a network E_x of points in the criterion space is obtained.

3rd stage (C). From the set of points E_x a Pareto subset E_x^p is separated.

4th stage (C). By examining the points of the set E_x^p non-empty orthants (i.e. orthants which contain points of the set E_x^p) are identified.

5th stage (MC). Each non-empty orthant is represented by a corresponding combination of five percent deflections from the threshold values for the criteria. The decision-maker ranks these combinations according to his preferences, thus ranking the orthants.

If the intersection of the set of all admissible alternatives D with the orthant A_j is small, it is highly probable that points of the network E_x will not occur in that intersection and will therefore be eliminated from any subsequent search. Because the most preferable alternative may be situated in this intersection, it is desirable to reduce the probability that it will be overlooked. This is the purpose of the sixth to ninth stages.

6th stage (C). Among the orthants which do not contain points of the set E_x^p those are sought in the vicinity of whose boundaries there are points of the set E_x^p. For this purpose each empty orthant, which is formed by intersection of the halfspaces $x_i \geq x_i^o$, $i \in Q_I$ and $x_j < x_j^o$, $j \in Q_2$, is associated with an expanded orthant created by intersection of the halfspaces $x_i \geq x_i^o + \Delta x_i$, $i \in Q_I$ and $x_j < x_j^o - \Delta x_j$, $j \in Q_2$ and then a check is made to determine whether this expanded orthant contains points of the set E_x^p.

7th stage (M). Among empty orthants the vicinity of whose boundaries contain points of the set E_x^p, those are identified whose ranks are at least equal to those non-empty orthants which have been identified at earlier stages.

8th stage (C). Points of the set E_x^p which are found in the vicinity of orthants which have been identified at the preceding stage. In the vicinities of the mapping of these points in the parameter space additional test points are generated.

9th stage (C). The criterion values are computed for these points and in this way a series, S_x, of additional points in the criteria space is obtained (2nd stage operation). From the set of points $R_x = E_x^p \cup S_x$ a Pareto subset R_x^p is separated (3rd stage operation). A check is made to see whether points of the series S_x have entered the orthants identified at the 7th stage.

10th stage (M). Among non-empty orthants (i.e. those that contain points of the set R_x^p) an orthant is identified which has the highest (first) rank (5th stage operation).

11th stage. The most preferable alternative in the non-empty orthant of the first rank is sought. For this purpose method [7] is used. This method uses the information received from the decision-maker in the form of ranking of increments. The decision-maker ranks five percent increments from criterion values in the i-th search point. The ranking obtained is then used to construct a cone of directions which is used to find the i+1-st search point. In order to find it, a series of test points are generated in the vicinity of the i-th search point in the parameter space. Then the one whose image in the criterion space hits the cone of directions is extracted.

12th stage (MC). The objective of this stage is rejection of those orthants whitin which points of the set R_x^p are much inferior, in terms of usefulness, than point $x^+(A_I)$, which was found in the preceding stage, and to identify areas which may contain more preferable points than $x^+(A_I)$. To do so, certain operations have to be carried out.

For each non-empty orthant A_j the vector of most preferable values $x^p(A_j)$ is computed whose i-th component ($i = 1, n$) is equal to the most preferable (the highest or the lowest) value of the i-th criterion among the versions found in this orthant. Because the system of preferences is monotone, this vector is superior, in terms of usefulness to all the alternatives contained in this othant (it is a sort of upper bound for these alternatives). The decison-maker compares the vector $x^p(A_j)$ with the vector $x^+(A_I)$. If the vector $x^p(A_j)$ is found to be less valuable than the vector $x^+(A_I)$, then all the alternatives which belong to the orthant A_j are inferior, in terms of usefulness, to the alternative $x^+(A_I)$. In this case the orthant A_j is rejected.

If the vector $x^p(A_j)$ is at least equal to the vector in terms of utility, then more accurate estimates of alternatives that belong to the orthan A_j are constructed. The range of the criterion X_I for the alternatives in the orthant A_j is divided into three equal intervals. In this way the set $R_X^p(A_j)$ of alternatives belonging to the orthant A_j is divided into three subsets. For each of these subsets a vector of most preferable values is computed. These vectors are compared with the vector $x^+(A_I)$. As a result some of the subsets are rejected and the others are further split up through division of the range of the criterion X_2, then of the criterion X_3, etc. The division process continues until the number of subsets (squares) reaches a specified number. Division and estimation in the orthant A_j results in rejection of either the entire set of alternatives belonging to this orthant or of some of them. Squares remain withing which there may be alternatives whose utility is superior of the alternative $x^+(A_I)$. In these squares the most preferable alternatives are sought (11th stage operation). The resultant most preferable alternatives are compared with the version $x^+(A_I)$. If one of them is found to be more preferable, then it is regarded as the reference instead of the alternative $x^+(A_I)$ in any subsequent search.

An analogous estimation and division process is carried out in the other non-empty orthants until the most preferable alternative is obtained for the entire set of objects of choice.

4. REFERENCES

1 Artobolevskiy, I.I. - S.V. Emelyanov V.I. Sergeev - O.A. Shestakov - R.B. Statnikov — An interactive Method for Optimal Machine Design. Doklady AN SSSR, Vol. 237, No. 4, 1977, pp. 793-796.

2 Huber G.P. — Multi-Attribute Utility Models: a Review of Field and Field-Like Studies; Management Science, vol. 20, No. 10, June 1974, pp. 1393-1401.

3 Larichev, O.I. - O.A. Polyakov — Interactive Procedures of Solving Multi-Criteria Mathematical Programming Problems (Survey). Ekonomika i matematicheske metody, Vol. 26, No. 1, 1980, pp. 129-145.

4 Shestakov, O.A. — Methods of Revealing Continuous Individual Preferences. In: Multi-Criteria Decision Making Problems. Mashinostroenie, Moscow, pp. 83-96.

5 Emelyanov, S.V. - V.I. Sergeev - S.I. Fridman - O.A. Shestakov — Choice of Optimal Machine Parameters through Qualitative Expert Evaluation. In: Computer Investigation of Machine Dynamics. Nauka, Moscow, 1980, pp. 3-8.

6 Sobol, I.M. — Uniformly Distributed Sequences with Additional Uniformity Properties. ZhVMMF, V. 16, No. 15, 1976, pp. 1332-1337.

THEORY AND PRACTICE OF
MULTIPLE CRITERIA DECISION MAKING
C. Carlsson and Y. Kochetkov (editors)

A SAMPLING-SEARCH-CLUSTERING APPROACH FOR SOLVING SCALAR (LOCAL, GLOBAL) AND VECTOR OPTIMIZING PROBLEMS

A. TÖRN
Åbo Akademi
Fänriksgatan 3, SF-20500 Åbo 50, Finland

ABSTRACT

An approach for analysing objective functions under quite general conditions is presented. The problems may either be constrained or unconstrained. The method does not put any restrictions on to the functional form of the objective function or the constraints. This means, for example, that the objective function could be multimodal and that the feasible region could be non-connected. The approach can also be extended to vector-valued objective functions. The basic ingredients used are multiple starting points, a local optimizer and a clustering analysis technique aiding in gaining efficiency and in displaying a global view of the problem analysed. The working of an algorithm implemented in Fortran is illustrated by some test problems. A nomography technique for visual presentation of the efficient solutions to MCDM problems is presented.

1 INTRODUCTION

Before discussing the concept of optimum solutions to problems involving multiple objectives and requirements on methods to assist in finding such optimum solutions, we define the meaning of some of the central terms used in multiple criteria analysis. [1]

1.1 Definitions

Attributes This term refers to descriptions of objective reality, which can be identified and measured relatively independently of the decision-maker's needs or desires.

Decision variables Those attributes, the values of which may be controlled by the decision-maker, are called the decision or control variables.

Decision space The space spanned by the decision variables is called the decision space. If we denote the spaces of the individual decision variables by X_i, $i=1, \ldots, n$ and the decision space by X then $X = X_1 \times X_2 \times \ldots \times X_m$.

Decision constraints The set of values that the decision attributes can obtain may be restricted by technological or other constraints. Let X^d be the subset of the decision space X where all these constraints are fulfilled. A point in X^d is a possible decision in the given decision situation.

Objectives Objectives are closely identifiable with a decision-maker's needs and desires; they represent directions of improvement or preference along individual attributes or functions of attributes. The space spanned by the objectives is called the space of objectives.

Goals Goals are fully identifiable with a decision-maker's needs and desires. They are a priori determined, specific values or levels defined in terms of other attributes of objectives.

Criteria Criteria are those decision constraints, obejctives, goals, and criteria constraints (further restricting the possible decisions X^d) that have been judged relevant in a given decision situation by a particular decision-maker (individual or group). We note that the criteria constraints are not as "hard" as the decision

1 Most of the definitions coincide with those of Zeleny (1982) [8]

constraints. The criteria constraints can be identified with desired levels of objectives and may be relaxed by lowering aspiration levels. Let X^c be the subset of X^d for which all criteria constraints are fulfilled. A point in X^c is a feasible decision in the given decision situation.

Let Y^d and Y^c be the sets corresponding to X^d and X^c in the space of objectives. A point in Y^d is called a possible alternative and a point in Y^c a feasible alternative.

1.2 Optimum solution

Let us now turn to the question of an optimum solution. The decision problems can be divided into two non-overlapping classes with respect to the optimality concept.

Scalar optimization problems The first class consists of the problems where the criteria consist of constraints restricting the set of feasible decisions in the given decision situation and a single scalar-valued objective function that is to be maximized or minimized on this set. In this case all decisions have been made prior to the solution process by specifying the constraints and the objective function and in principle the solution process will be purely mechanical. This does not mean that the solution process should be trivial; it may be difficult not only to find an optimum solution but in some cases even to find any solution or establish whether an obtained solution is optimum or not. For example, the set of feasible decisions X^c may be empty or non-connected and the objective function may be multimodal on this set.

The scalar optimization problems may further be divided into two classes; local optimization problems and global optimization problems. The objective function of the former class of problems is unimodal in X^c, whereas for the later class of problems it is multimodal. Most of the research effort in optimization has been spent on designing methods guaranteeing optimum solutions to problems belonging to sub-classes of local optimization problems. Lately (Dixon & Szegö [1]) some effort has been spent on designing methods for global optimization problems. Most or these problems are inconvenient from a theoretical point of view because of the non-existence of methods guaranteeing the discovery of an optimum solution.

Guaranteeing a solution means that the decision-maker can be P = 100 percent confident that the optimum solution has been obtained. The best that can be done in global optimization is to determine a solution with confidence $P = P_g < 100$ where

P_g is determined by the decision-maker. In section 2 where a global optimization method is presented we return to this confidence concept in more detail.

Vector optimization problems The second class consists of problems for which the criteria contain several scalar-valued objective functions to be optimized simultaneously. Here the definition of an optimum solution must be extended. In the criteria formulation the Pareto optimum solutions $Y^e \subset Y^c$ (also termed the non-dominated solutions or the efficient surface) are all optimum because none of these are dominated by any other alternative in Y^c. The task of determining Y^e is thus a global optimization problem. In order to extract a point in Y^e as the optimum solution information not contained in the criteria must be used unless Y^e exceptionally contains a single point, the so -called ideal. The choice of a single point from Y^e is of course dependent on which points are available, i.e., of Y^e. This means that the solution process consists of two steps. First, the criteria are formulated giving the set of optimum solutions Y^e of the criteria problem. Second, the points in Y^e are taken as the feasible solutions and by externally evaluating these the final choice (decision) can be made.

The external evaluation is made by the aid of some normally implicit utility function existing in the mind of the decision-maker. This function may partly depend on important factors unsuitable for representation as criteria in the criteria formulation of the problem.

The optimization situation in the second step is characterized by the following. The implicit utility function may be multimodal on Y^e. This is true, for example, if Y^e is a non-connected set (For an example of such a case, see sample problem in Fig. 3b). This means that some global optimization technique should be applied. The confidence requirement of global optimization normally means that a large number of utility function evaluations have to be performed. However, as the function must be evaluated by the decision-maker, normally by rank ordering solutions, only a very moderate number of evaluations can be made. This requires that the solutions in Y^e be aggregated in some way to ease the evaluation burden of the decision-maker.

1.3 Requirements on MCDM methods

Based on the foregoing discussion the following conclusions are made. A minimum requirement on a MCDM method is that it should give at least one optimum solution with specified confidence. Normally it will be required that a representative sample of the optimum solutions be obtained. Also non-optimum solutions may be of interest for the decision-maker because of the information they provide about the problem.

Methods for scalar optimization Many MCDM problems formulated as scalar optimization problems are global optimization problems and for many others it will not be known whether they are global or local optimization problems. In order to be generally usable the method should therefore be able to solve global optimization problems. Further, there should be few requirements regarding the functional form of the constraints and the objective function.

Methods for vector optimization These methods should be able to determine a representative sample Y_s^e of the efficient surface Y^e and to present Y_s^e in an aggregated way for the decision-maker. The methods should also permit the decision-maker to explore Y^e in more detail in the vicinity of interesting sample solutions.

The rest of the paper is devoted to the presentation of methods for solution of MCDM problems. In section 2 a global optimization method is presented and in section 3 a vector optimization method based on the method given in section 2 is presented. In section 4 the possibilities of using nomography tools for displaying solutions in an aggregated way is explored.

2 A GLOBAL OPTIMIZATION METHOD

2.1 Basic approach

Given a region $A = X^c \sqsubset \mathbb{R}^m$ and a function $f : A \rightarrow \mathbb{R}$, a global minimum of f in A is to be determined. The objective function f may be multimodal in A so that many local minima may exist. Assuming the existence of a set $M \sqsubset A$, where f obtains its minimum

$$M = \{ x^* \varepsilon A : f(x^*) \leq f(x), \forall x \varepsilon A \}$$

the problem can be stated as "determine a point in M". Because numerical algorithms are used it is usually impossible to expect to determine a point in M but in $M \sqsupset M_\varepsilon$ where

$$M_\varepsilon = \{ x \varepsilon A ; f(x) - f^* < \varepsilon , f^* = f(x^*) \} \tag{2.1}$$

A point in $M\varepsilon$ can therefore be considered a solution to the problem. There exist classes of problems for small m (usually $m \leq 2$) which can be solved in a finite number of steps by certain deterministic algorithms. For most problems, no method exists with guaranteed convergence to a solution at feasible cost. For such problems it would be desirable to use a method that would obtain a good estimate at a given computational cost. The decision as to which method is preferred must then be based on the probabilities of obtaining certain levels of the objective function. In a practical situation it is also important to obtain some stopping condition related to the expected quality of the estimate.

One of the most frequently used approaches to global optimization is the multistart algorithm (MS). The following observation is the motive for our attempts to design a class of better models: when starting from several randomly sampled points (global points), the local optimizer used in MS will normally arrive at the same local solution several times. This means that much of the effort spent on global optimization is unnecessary re-determination of a local solution that has already been found, whereas this effort could be spent on exploring more global points and thus increasing the probability of arriving at a global solution.

In our algorithm a clustering analysis technique is used to prevent multiple determination of a local solution. A few steps of the local optimizer can be expected to gather the points around the local solutions so that clusters of points will emerge. With the aid of the clustering analysis technique these clusters can then be recognized and a reduction of the points leading to the same local solution can be made.

Based on the foregoing reasoning the following model for global optimization is formulated.

Algorithm MSC (Multistart with clustering)

1 [Global points] Choose global points.

2 [Local search] Push the points some steps towards the local optima by using a local optimizer.

3 [Find clusters] Find clusters by using a clustering analysis technique. If a tolerance condition is met, stop.

4 [Reduce points] Take a sample of points from each cluster. Return to step 2.

2.2 Probability of finding a global solution

The probability of finding a global solution depends on how many starting points are used.

The number of points N that need to be sampled initially could be determined on the basis of the following reasoning. In order to obtain the global maximum, at least one starting point leading to the global maximum should be sampled. Let us assume that the probability of finding such a point when sampling one point at random in A is p. Then if N points are sampled independently, the probability $1 - \varepsilon$ of obtaining at least one point leading to the global maximum is given by

$$1 - \varepsilon = 1 - (1 - p)^N.$$

Solving for N gives

$$N_c = [\ln \varepsilon / \ln (1 - p)] \tag{2.2}$$

By assuming the size of p and choosing ε, N can be computed. The probability of finding the global maximum could be increased by using stratified sampling instead of random sampling. For stratified sampling the hyperrectangle H can be divided into parts and we obtain (A is divided into q identical parts) $N \cong N_s$ where

$$N_s = [q \ln \varepsilon / \ln (1 - qp)], \tag{2.3}$$

if the assumption that the points leading to the global maximum are approximately contained in one of the q parts is true. If $q = N_s$, i.e. one point is sampled in each part q, we obtain

$$N_s = [(1 - \varepsilon)/p]. \tag{2.4}$$

For $\varepsilon = p = 0{,}05$, $q = N_s$ we obtain $N_c = 59$, $N_s = 19$ and for $\varepsilon = p = 0.01$, $q = N_s$ we have $N_c = 459$, $N_s = 99$.

2.3 Details of the algorithm

Starting points The aim of determining the choice of starting points should be to obtain starting points leading to a global maximum. If no a priori information about the location of the global maximum is available, all parts of A should be treated as equally important when sampling the starting points. MSC also permits guesses to be submitted. In order to obtain starting points in A the region A is circumscribed by a hyperrectangle H. Sampling is then performed in H, and the points falling within A are taken as starting points.

Local search The choice of local optimizer is critical for MS and MSC when the cost of a global optimization is considered. This is because most of the time will be spent in using the local optimizer. A good choice may, however, require some a priori information about the function f and the region A. If no a priori information about f and A is assumed to be available, then a method that works under general conditions could be used. The method implement here is a method named UNIRANDI.

UNIRANDI, as used here, consists of the two elements random search and linear search. Random search means that a line (direction determined at random) is laid through the base point. If one of the two points on that line at distance d from the base point is better than the base point a linear search is performed in the first promising direction. If two lines are tried without success the distance d is halved and a new random search is started. Linear search means that points at distances 2d, 4d, 8d, ..., 2^kd on the line are tried as long as better and better points are obtained. The best point at distance 2^kd from the base point is then taken as the new base point and a new random search is started with steplength d = 2^{k-1}d.

The lack of sophistication of UNIRANDI does not necessarily mean that the method is always inferior to a more sophisticated method. For a number of test problems the performance of UNIRANDI was better than that of a method of the variable metric type, see Gomulka, 1978 [2].

Find clusters Cluster analysis techniques are used in various scientific areas for dividing a finite set of objects or points into subsets so that each object is more similar to objects within its subset than to the objects outside. We shall assume that the objects can be represented as points in the M-dimensional Euclidean space and that the deviance (square of the Euclidean distance) is used as the dissimilarity measure.

A class of clustering techniques which does not necessarily requires that the whole dissimilarity measure matrix be computed is the technique of growing a cluster from a centre or a seed point. Classification procedures using this technique can be expected to give satisfactory results for hyperspherical and well-separated clusters. One problem that has to be solved when using such a technique is how to locate the seed points. Another problem which is common to most classification procedures is the choice of some condition (threshold distance) for stopping the growth of a cluster. The choice of the threshold distance r is critical because if r is very large, all the poins will be assigned to a single cluster and if r is very small, each point will form an isolated cluster.

The preordering of the points in accordance with their suitability as seed points is performed by sorting them in descending order with respect to the corresponding function values. The assumption made is that the local maxima would be good seed points to use and that the point with the largest function value may be taken as an estimate of a local maximum. Therefore when a new seed point is needed the point, among those not yet classified, with the largest value is chosen.

For further details of the cluster analysis algorithm, see Törn, 1977 [5].

The clustering can be made either in the decision space (M = m) or in the space of objectives (M = 1). In the first case, similar decisions will be clustered, whereas in the second case similar consequences will be grouped. Both approaches will be illustrated in the next section.

Reduction of points In order that a large number of global points may be used to increase the probability of obtaining a solution, the points which are pushed towards the local solutions should be reduced during the iterations of MSC. The number of points should be reduced in such a way that not all the points leading to a solution, of any are present, are rejected. Of course, this cannot generally be guaranteed and the probability of success will also depend on the specific problem and on steps two and three in MSC. If the foregoing steps were successful, it would be sufficient to choose one point from each recognized cluster in order to guarantee a solution. In general, at least one point from each cluster should therefore be chosen. If more than one point is chosen from a cluster, the motive for this is to assure that any cluster found really consists of points leading to a unique local solution. The points should therefore be chosen to test this as well as possible. One natural way would be to use cluster analysis for the points in each cluster to obtain subclusters and then choose one point from each subcluster. Another way would be to rank the points in each cluster in descending order of function values and then choose every second, third or so in the hope that function values corresponding to poins leading to a lower local optimum would also be smaller. This technique has been implemented.

Normally the number of clusters obtained during the cycles will be greater than or equal to the number of existing local maxima. This means that it should be sufficient to consider only one search process from each cluster for the next cycle. As already stated above, the reason for choosing more than one process from a cluster is the suspicion that processes in the same cluster will lead to different local maxima. This may occur if some local maxima are very close to each other. By close is here meant close in the decision space or close in the space of objectives dependent on the space in which clustering is performed. However, even if only one process is chosen from such a cluster, there is a good chance that the best maximum will be detected because the process with the largest function value is chosen.

MSC is written in standard FORTRAN IV. It consists of a main program GLOPT and 14 subprograms. Two of these, the testing of ε A and the computation of f(x) must be written by the user. For further details of the programs, see Törn, 1979 [6].

2.2 Numerical illustrations

In order to illustrate the working of MSC the following problem is used

Problem 1 The object function [1] is

$$f(x_1, x_2) = x_1^2 + (x_2 - 2)^2 - 7 \tag{2.5}$$

and the restricting region A is determined by the inequalities

$$A : \begin{cases} -x_1^3 + x_1^2 + x_1 - x_2 + 1 \leq 0 \\ (x_1 + 3)^2 + (x_2 - 2)^2 - 36 \leq 0 \\ -(x_1 + 3)^2 - (x_2 - 6)^2 + 16 \leq 0 \end{cases} \tag{2.6}$$

The function f has four local maxima $P_1, P_2, \ldots, P_4$ all on the boundary of A (see Fig. 1).

---

1 This problem is dealt with by Pfranger 1970 [3].

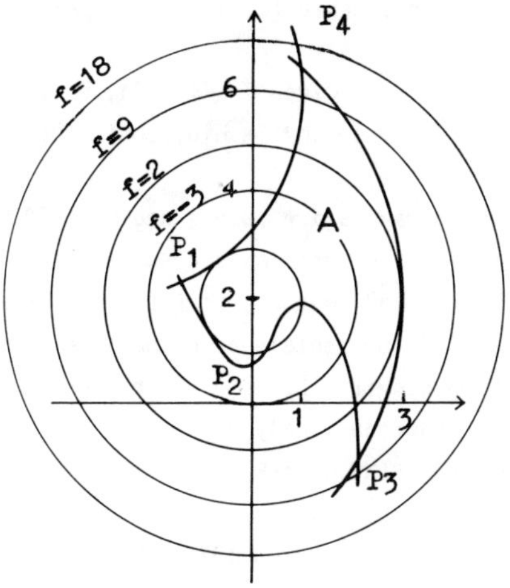

Fig. 1. Problem 1. Local maxima P_1, P_2, P_3, P_4. Global maximum P_4.

The coordinates and the corresponding function values (given to 3 decimal places) are

$$P_1 = \begin{pmatrix} -1.107 \\ 2.476 \end{pmatrix}, \ f(P_1) = -5.547 \quad P_3 = \begin{pmatrix} 2.036 \\ -1.261 \end{pmatrix}, \ f(P_3) = 7,782$$

$$P_2 = \begin{pmatrix} -0.416 \\ 0.829 \end{pmatrix}, \ f(P_2) = -5.456 \quad P_4 = \begin{pmatrix} 0.969 \\ 6.500 \end{pmatrix}, \ f(P_4) = 14.188. \tag{2.7}$$

Further, there is a number of boundary points for which the gradient of f is at right angles to the boundary and directed outwards from it. This means that when such a boundary point or a nearby point is reached in the local search process, further progress may no be possible. This is especially true for the point $P_5 = (3.\ 2)^T$, $f(P_5) = 2$.

The sampling of starting points is done by taking points uniformly distributed in the rectangle H

$$H \ : \begin{cases} -4 \leq x_1 \leq 4 \\ -4 \leq x_2 \leq 4 \end{cases} \tag{2.8}$$

and choosing as starting points those falling within A.

Sample output from the program is given in Fig. 2a, b. In Fig. 2a the clustering is performed in the decision space and in Fig. 2b in the f-space.

In the first case all local maxima are found, see CLUSTERING 2 in Fig. 2a; the maxima are well separated in the decision space, see Fig. 1. In the second case P_1 and P_2 are not well separated in the criteria space because $f(P_1) = f(P_2)$, see (2.7) and they will therefore be contained in the same cluster, see CLUSTERING 1 in Fig. 2b. (The global points are the same as in Fig. 2a). If the best point from each cluster is permitted continue, only one of the points P_1 and P_2 will be found, in this sample P_2, see CLUSTERING 2 in Fig. 2b.

For other illustrations of MSC see Dixon 1978 [1].

3 VECTOR OPTIMIZING

3.1 Statement of problem

Let $X \sqsubset \mathbb{R}^m$ be the space of control or decision variables, i.e. $\forall x \in X$, $x = (x_1, x_2, \ldots, x_m)$ and let $X^c \sqsubset X$ be the set of feasible x's determined by a set of linear or non-linear inequalities. Let $g_1, g_2, \ldots, g_n$ be be the objective functions $X^c \rightarrow \mathbb{R}^1$, each function evaluating some important objective of a feasible decision. Let $y(x)$ be the vector $(g_1(x), g_2(x), \ldots, g_n(x)$. Then the feasible set of alternatives Y^c is defined by

$$Y^c = \{ y(x) : x \in X_o \}. \tag{3.1}$$

For some problems just a number of feasible alternatives $y_k = (g_{1k}, g_{2k}, \ldots, g_{nk})$, $k \in K = \{1, 2, \ldots,\}$ are given. The $Y^c = \{ y_1, y_2, \ldots, y_N \}$.

We can now state the MCDM problem P1:
Find

$$x^* \in X^c \quad \text{such that} \quad y^* = (g_1(x^*), g_2(x^*), \ldots, g_n(x^*)) \tag{P1}$$

is the optimum alternative in Y^c. If explicit alternatives are given, the problem is to choose the optimum alternative $y \in Y^c$.

GLOBAL POINTS

NAME	F	X1	X2
1	.448505+00	.225678+01	.353475+01
2	-.594867+01	-.964401+00	.234822+01
3	.216099+01	.295050+01	.132508+01
4	-.595688+01	-.166608+00	.300765+01
5	-.546897+01	-.454239+00	.849045+00
6	-.428411+00	.212689+01	.568940+00
7	.462681+00	.263904+01	.129420+01
8	-.643439+01	.399960+00	.263690+01
9	-.758404+00	.158947+01	.392748+01
10	-.328669+01	.179409+01	.129676+01

CLUSTERING 1

FUNCTION EVALUATIONS 79
NUMBER OF POINTS 10
NUMBER OF CLUSTERS 4
DIMENSIONALITY OF SPACE 2
THRESHOLD .109+01

CLUST	NAME	SAME	FROM	EVAL	F	X1	X2
1	4		0	14	.666837+01	.173881+01	.526266+01
1	9		0	11	.625526+01	.226892+01	.484733+01
1	8		0	18	.525451+01	.239063+01	.455723+01
1	1		0	9	.438206+01	.242231+01	.434829+01
2	6		0	4	.235459+01	.257973+01	.356952+00
2	3	SAME	0	3	.216099+01	.295050+01	.132508+01
2	7	SAME	0	3	.462631+00	.263904+01	.129420+01
2	10		0	11	.133000+01	.286730+01	.167044+01
3	5	SAME	0	3	-.546897+01	-.454239+00	.849045+00
4	2	SAME	0	3	-.594867+01	-.964401+00	.234822+01

CLUSTERING 2

FUNCTION EVALUATIONS 141
NUMBER OF POINTS 4
NUMBER OF CLUSTERS 4
DIMENSIONALITY OF SPACE 2
THRESHOLD .109+01

CLUST	NAME	SAME	FROM	EVAL	F	X1	X2	
1	4		1	33	.140649+02	.983297+00	.648308+01	P_4
2	6		2	31	.499300+01	.249947+01	-.397006+00	P_3
3	5	SAME	3	8	-.546897+01	-.454239+00	.849045+00	P_2
4	2		4	14	-.571164+01	-.100301+01	.253134+01	P_1

Fig. 2a. Sample output from the MSC algorithm for problem 1. Clustering in decision space (X-space).

CLUSTERING 1

FUNCTION EVALUATIONS 79
NUMBER OF POINTS 10
NUMBER OF CLUSTERS 6
DIMENSIONALITY OF SPACE 1
THRESHOLD .842+00

CLUST	NAME	SAME	FROM	EVAL	F	X1	X2	
1	4		0	14	.666837+01	.173881+01	.526266+01	
1	9		0	11	.625526+01	.226892+01	.484733+01	
2	8		0	18	.525451+01	.239063+01	.455723+01	
3	1		0	9	.438206+01	.242231+01	.434829+01	
4	6		0	4	.235459+01	.257973+01	.356952+00	
4	3	SAME	0	3	.216099+01	.295050+01	.132508+01	
4	10		0	11	.133000+01	.286730+01	.167044+01	
5	7	SAME	0	3	.462631+00	.263904+01	.129420+01	
6	5	SAME	0	3	-.546897+01	-.454239+00	.849045+00	P_2
6	2	SAME	0	3	-.594867+01	-.964401+00	.234822+01	P_1

CLUSTERING 2

FUNCTION EVALUATIONS 158
NUMBER OF POINTS 6
NUMBER OF CLUSTERS 5
DIMENSIONALITY OF SPACE 1
THRESHOLD .842+00

CLUST	NAME	SAME	FROM	EVAL	F	X1	X2	
1	4		1	33	.140649+02	.983297+00	.648308+01	P_4
1	1		3	31	.136353+02	.104380+01	.642107+01	
2	8		2	27	.527382+01	.243776+01	.451618+01	→ P_4
3	6		4	16	.402282+01	.264474+01	-.702697-02	P_3
4	7		5	15	.220658+01	.295647+01	.131747+01	→ P_3
5	5	SAME	6	8	-.546897+01	-.454239+00	.849045+00	P_2

Fig. 2b. Sample output from the MSC algorithm for problem 1. Clustering in the criteria space (F-space).

3.2 Approaches to solution

The solution process would ideally be some interaction between the DM and a computerized decision aid (DA). With the information given in the problem formulation P1 above, the DM has to be asked whether one alternative is preferred to another. The only task that the DA can perform is to provide feasible alternatives.

In order to be able to shift more of the burden on to the DA, standardized objective functions f_i corresponding to the objective functions g_i are introduced. These permit automatic decisions to be made insofar as $f_i(x_2^1) > f_i(x^2)$ always means that the consequence $g_i(x^1)$ is preferred to $g_i(x^2)$. In many cases we would have $f_i(x) = g_i(x)$ but in some cases a transformation of g_i is necessary in order to obtain the corresponding f_i. Letting $z(x) = (f_1(x), f_2(x), \ldots, f_n(x))$ we can define Z^c analogously to Y^c, namely as

$$Z^c = \{z(x) : x \in X^c\}. \tag{3.2}$$

With objective functions given, Pareto optimum or efficient alternatives can be determined by the DA. Let us denote this approach P2.

A further step is to introduce utility functions. These are combined in some manner so that a one-dimensional objective function U

$$U(x) = U(u_1(x), u_2(x), \ldots, u_n(x)) \tag{3.3}$$

is obtained. With U given (approach P3), the DA could in principle find the optimum decision. MCDM methods used in approaches P1 and P2 are called interactive methods because of the interaction between the DA and the DM in the solution process. Methods used in P3 are called multiattribute utility (MAU) methods.

For problems with a scalar utility function the algorithm MSC could be used. In the next section we shall see how a modification of MSC could be used to tackle problems of type P2.

3.3 A modification of MSC for vector optimizing

Determining a set of efficient alternatives Y^e. For P2 level problems the efficient alternatives can in principle be determined. First, N points are sampled at random in X_0 in the same way as for P1 level problems. Each of the N points in X^c

is now in turn taken as a starting point for a local optimizer, the task of which is to push the corresoponding point in Y^c towards the efficient surface Y^e. The local optimizer used is UNIRANDI described in section 2.3.

Let us now assume that the N points are on the efficient surface (e.g. within a small distance of the efficient surface) after using the local optimizer. We next discuss how the sample Y_s^e should be presented to the DM.

Presenting the sample Y_s^e, of Y^e to the DM. The information contained in the sample Y_s^e should now be presented to the DM so that a clear picture of Y^e is obtained. First, the points should be presented in some natural order. Second, becuase some of the points in Y_s^e may be very close to each other and thus represent roughly the same information, those points should be grouped into classes and the classes instead of the points be presented to the DM. By aggregating the information in this way it is hoped that the amount of data be considered will be reduced to manageable proportions even if the number of points N in Y_s^e is large.

Let us turn first to the question of the order in which to present the points. It would be natural to present them in ascending or descending order of one of the value functions f_i. If no objective is considered more important than another, a complete presentation containing all the n possible orderings could be produced.

In the grouping process a clustering algorithm could be used. For a cluster analysis algorithm to be used, a similarity measure must be defined, i.e. we must specify quantitatively the degree of closeness of any two points in Y_s^e. Two points that have almost the same numerical values for the value functions will of course be considered close. The closeness of two numerical values of a given value function is of course dependent on the size of the interval over which the value function varies for the points in Y_s^e. We therefore transform the points in Z_s^e by dividing each coordinate by the size of the variation interval of that coordinate and then take the square of the Euclidean distance, the deviance, as the dissimilarity measure.

The pre-ordering of the N points in Z_s^e according to their suitability as seed points is performed by ranking them in descending order according to the numerical values of one of the value functions f_i. This means that when a new seed point is needed, the point with the largest value of f_i among those not yet classified is chosen. In this way the question of the natural order of presentation of the points in the clustering process is solved.

Detailed analysis of Y^e near points in Y^e_s. The same steps 1-2 that are applied to obtain Y^e_s could be applied for detailed analysis of points in Y^e_s by specifying subregions of interest in X^c and Y^c. For example, if $y(x^s) \varepsilon Y^e_s$ is considered a promising solution, i.e. a decision with favourable consequences $(g_1(x^s),\ldots,g_n(x^s))$ then the sampling could be performed in a small hyperrectangle $H_s \subset H$ with x^s as the centre. Furthermore, the DM could supply additional constraints on the consequence variables such as $d^s_i < g_i(x) \leq D^s_i$ for some of the consequences or all, according to his own choice, in order to converge on the optimal solution. It would be possible to introduce some utility function for this detailed analysis because the DM would have relatively exact information regarding where in the range the consequence variable outcomes were prior to analysis. The order of presentation would then be in descending order of this utility function, which would also be used to order the seed points for the clustering algorithm.

Further refinement of the DA. In order to reduce the computational effort needed to obtain Y^e_s, the points finally reaching Y^e could be reduced by clustering the points iteratively during the local optimization process and by letting only a sample of points Y^k_s of all points Y^k be starting points for the local optimizer for the next iteration k + 1. This means that $\# Y^k \geq \# Y^k_s$, $\# Y^k_s = \# Y^{k+1}$. The set Y^k may contain points that are dominated by other points in Y^k and an obvious reduction would be to let Y^k_s contain only nondominated points. An iteration could be terminated and the points clustered when the step-length of the optimizer started from every starting point were reduced below a specified limit step-length d^k.

For some of the value functions f_i the maximum may be obtained on a ridge in X^c. This will happen for f_i if the control variables x_i are not all contained in the objective function f_i. If, when determining efficient solutions, the maximum of such a function f_i is obtained, the next dominating point will also be on the ridge and thus hard to find. One way to overcome this difficulty is to flatten out the top of the ridge by specifying an interval $(f_i - D_i, f_i)$ where the value of f_i is considered constant. The entity D_i could, for example, be specified as a given percentage of the whole variation interval of f_i over Y^k. This procedure will, in the presence of conflicting goals, make Y^k and also Y^e_s contain compromise solutions because the tops of the value functions will be cut. This should not make the set Y^e_s less representative.

On the contrary, as the optimal solution will normally be a compromise solution, the compromise set Y^e_s will be even more useful than an unbiased set Y^e_s. It would also be possible to use the entities D_i for introducing trade-offs between the attribute functions by specifying the percentage part of D_i differently for different attribute functions.

We next summarize the discussion in this section by showing details of the algorithm, see algorithm MSCM.

Algorithm MSCM (Multistart with clustering algorithm for solving MCDM problems)

1. Determine a sample of points Y_s^e of the efficient surface Y^e
   - 1.1 [Starting points] Obtain a set feasible starting points $X_s(Y_s)$, $X_s \sqsubset X^c$ by sampling in a hyperrectangle $H \sqsubset X^c$.
   - 1.2 [Y_s^e is determined iteratively over the sets Y^k, Y_s^k, k=0,1,..., with $Y_s^0 = Y_s$]
     - 1.2.1 [Local optimization] Push the points in Y_s^k some steps towards Y^e to obtain Y^{k+1} by using a local optimizer.
     - 1.2.2 [Find clusters] Find clusters in Y^{k+1} by using a cluster analysis technique.
     - 1.2.3 [Reduce points] Reduce the points in Y^{k+1} to obtain Y_s^{k+1}. Display summary of intermediate results.
     - 1.2.4 [Test for Y_s^e] When Y_s^e is obtained, go to step 2, otherwise repeat the steps 1.2.1 - 1.2.4 for next k.
2. [Display Y_s^e] Display Y_s^e, X_s^e and other summary information.
3. [Detailed analysis] For detailed analysis of interesting parts of Y^e, make necessary changes in the problem description and repeat the steps 1-3.

For further details see Törn, 1980 [7].

3.4 Numerical illustrations

Problem 2 The problem is described in Fig. 3a and b.

Utility function approach As an illustration let us solve problem 2 by using an utility function u. We shall assume that u has the following form:

$$- u(x) = ag_1(x) + g_2(x)$$

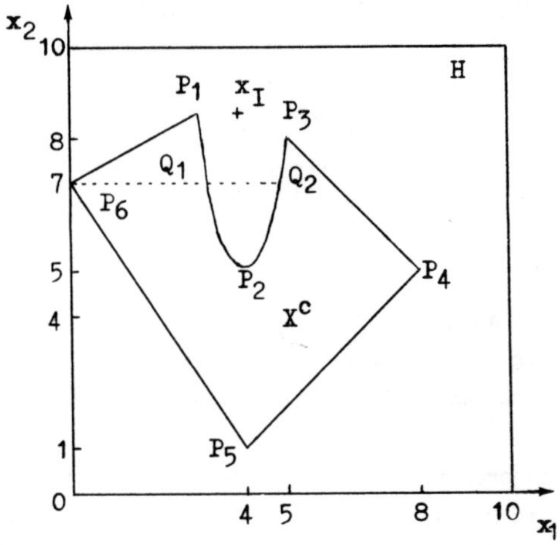

Fig. 3a. Feasible region X^c; Decision variables: x_1, x_2. Feasible decisions: X^c; P_1P_3 : $3(x_1-4)^2 - x_2 + 5 = 0$; P_3P_4: $- x_1 - x_2 + 13 = 0$; P_4P_5: $- x_1 + x_2 + 3 = 0$; P_5P_6: $3x_1 + 2x_2 - 14 = 0$; P_6P_1: $x_1 - 2x_2 + 14 = 0$; Ideal decision x_I: (4, 8.46281).

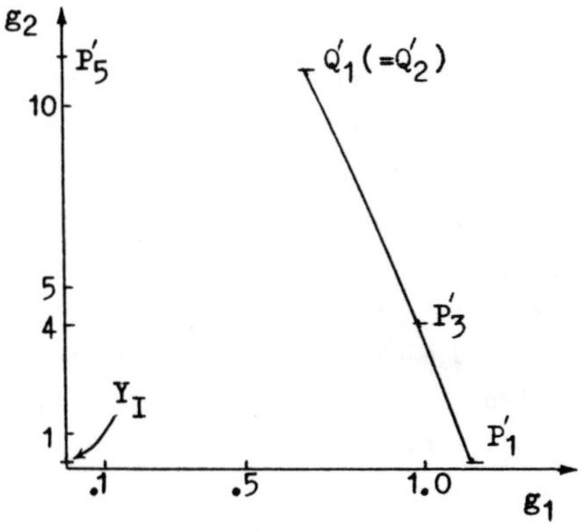

Fig. 3b. Efficient surface; Efficient surface Y^e: $Q_1'P_1'$ (Q_1' excluded) and P_5'; Objective functions $g_1(x) = (x_1 - 4)^2$; $g_2(x) = 20 - (x_2 - 4)^2$; Standaridized objective functions $f_1(x) = -g_1(x)$, $f_2(x) = - g_2(x)$, i.e., max (f_1, f_2); Ideal y_I: (0, 0.83285).

Then we have the following possible solutions ot the problem max u(x), s.t. $x \varepsilon X^c$

parameter range	local optima	global optimum
$0 \leq a \leq 6$	P_1, P_2, P_5	P_1
$6 < a < 15$	P_1, P_2, P_3, P_5	$P_1(a<9.6)$, $P_5(a>9.6)$
$15 \leq a < 16.3$	P_1, P_2, P_5	P_5
$16.4 < a \leq \infty$	P_2, P_5	P_5

We note that the solution is given by the choice of a and that the optimization problem for each a is a global optimization problem. We also note that only a few points of the efficient surface will be obtained in this utility function approach.

<u>Experiments with MSCM algorithm</u> In the experiment 64 points were obtained in X^c by stratified sampling in H. ($N_s = q = 64$, $\varepsilon = p = 1/65 \approx 0.0154$ in (2.3)). In Fig. 4 the results from the second and third pass through the steps 1.2.1 - 1.2.3 in the algorithm are shown. The 6 clusters, containing 14 points in all, can be said to give a good representation of the efficient surface, i.e. of the possible solutions to the problem. In the clustering algorithm the covariance matrix of the points in Y^k is needed and therefore the correlation matrix can be computed without much extra cost. The correlation coefficients will give some indication of the degree of conflict in the attributes.

For the third clustering the coefficient is -0.85, i.e. indicates that the objective functions almost linearly conflict over the efficient surface. This can also be seen from Fig. 4b. The value function $f_1(x)$ obtains its maximum value 0 in X^c on the ridge $x_1 = 4$. Without any ridge prevention technique, points will be captured on this ridge (Törn 1976). In the experiment the points were permitted to deviate by up to 5% of the variation interval of the functions f_1 and f_2 from their estimated maxima, which was enough to prevent the points from being captured on the ridge. The passes 4-7 through the steps 1.2.1 - 1.2.3 did not change the result in Fig. 4b substantially; the same number of clusters with the same number of points were obtained. This means that the points at the end of pass 3 have approximately arrived at their Y^e positions and that the iteration could be stopped after the forth pass, the first pass giving the same number of points and clusters as an immediately previous pass. The test in step 1.2.4 of the algorithm could be based on this reasoning. The whole analysis for the seven passes took 4 sec of CPU time on a UNIVAC 1108 computer.

In Fig. 5 the output from MSCM corresponding to Fig. 4b is shown.

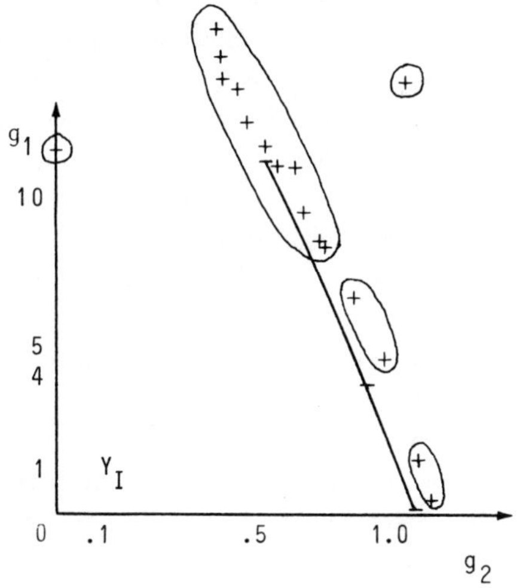

Fig. 4a. Results from second pass:22 dominating points, 10 clusters (5 outside the figure), 872 function evaluations.

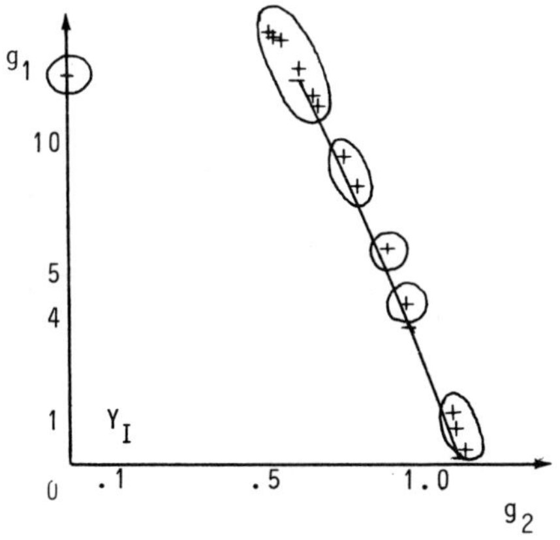

Fig. 4b. Results from third pass:14 dominating points. 6 clusters, 1426 function evaluations.

4. EFFICIENT SURFACE PRESENTATION USING NOMOGRAPHY

The presentation of the efficient surface (or a representative sample thereof) in such a way that the decision-maker obtains a good picture of the choices available is an important problem in MCDM. The solution to this problem presented in section 3 was to group similar solutions with the aid of a clustering method and to present representatives of the groups rather than all efficient solutions. In this section we shall illustrate the use of nomography to present the efficient solutions. We use problem 2 described in section 3.4. Of course, there is no need to use nomography if the number of objective functions is 2. In this case the efficient solutions are best presented as in Fig. 4. In order to illustrate the possibilities of nomography we extend the objective functions to include x_1 and x_2.

In Fig. 5 one part of the efficient surface of the extended problem is presented by a sparse nomogram. Each line in the nomogram represents one efficient solution by showing the values of the objective functions x_1, x_2, g_1 and g_2. The nomogram gives quite a good picture of this part of the efficient surface. By interpolating between nomogram lines new approximate efficient solutions may be discovered. For a further illustration of the technique see Instructors Manual to Zeleny 1982 [8]

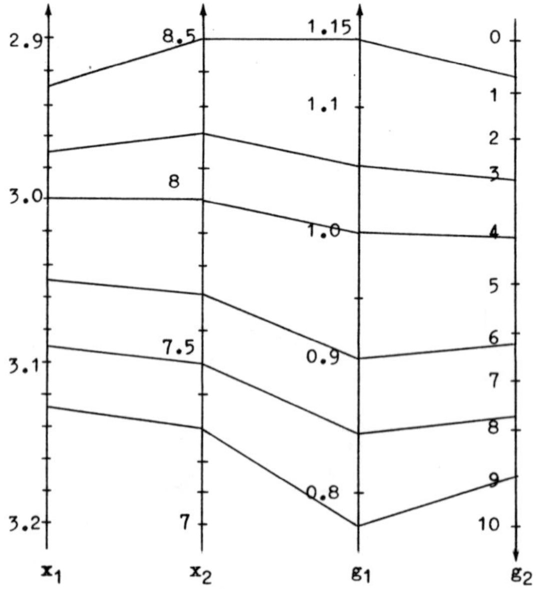

Fig. 5. Nomogram representation of part of the efficient surface of problem 2.

CONCLUSIONS

The optimization tool presented can be applied to a large range of optimization problems. It has been successfully applied to problems with multimodal objective functions. A large amount of extra information about the optimization problem may be extracted from the output of the algorithm. This makes the algorithm very useful as a first tool for analyzing optimization problems.

REFERENCES

1 Dixon, L.C.W. - G.P. Szegö (eds.) Towards Global Optimization, Vol. 2, North-Holland, Amsterdam, 1978.

2 Gomulka, J. A user's experience with Törn's clustering algorithm, in Dixon and Szegö (Eds.), 1978, pp 63-70.

3 Pfranger, P. Ein heuristisches Verfahren zur globalen Optimierung, Unternehmensforschung 14, 1970, pp 27-50.

4 Törn, A.A. Mathematical programming methods for multiple criteria decision making: An analysis and some suggestions, FEI Working Paper 26, 1978.

5 Törn, A.A. Cluster analysis using seed points and density-determined hyperspheres as an aid to global optimization. IEEE Trans. Systems Man and Cybernetics, Vol. SMC-7, No. 8, 1977, pp 610-616.

6 Törn, A.A. A program for global optimization, Multistart with clustering (MSC), Proceedings of Euro IFIP 79, P.A. Sonnet (Ed.), North-Holland, 1979, pp 427-434.

7 Törn, A.A. A sampling-search-clustering approach for exploring the feasible/efficient solutions of MCDM problems, Comput. & Oper. Res., Vol. 7, 1980, pp 67-79.

8 Zeleny, M. Multiple Criteria Decision Making, McGraw-Hill, New York, 1982.

THEORY AND PRACTICE OF
MULTIPLE CRITERIA DECISION MAKING
C. Carlsson and Y. Kochetkov (editors)

INTERACTIVE SYSTEMS RESULTING FROM A DESCRIPTIVE APPROACH TO THE SOLUTION OF COMPLEX ILL-STRUCTURED PROBLEMS

S.V. KHAYNISH, A.G. VLASOV

International Research Institute for Management Sciences
Shepkina Street 8, Moscow 129090 USSR

ABSTRACT

The paper is concerned with the principles involved in the design of interactive systems intended to solve the complex ill-structured problems which are extensively encountered in management systems.

Interactive systems can be obtained by means of a descriptive approach whereby the dialogue scenario is developed using a descriptive model of the problem-solver's behaviour. For ordering the objects, resource allocation and planning, interactive systems DISIOR, DISIOR-RESOURCE and DISIOR-SPEKTR have been developed. A detailed account of the second is given. Interactive systems which rely on several programming languages have been implemented as software in various computers and are intended both for training managers and more effective planning and managerial processes.

1. A CLASS OF COMPLEX ILL-STRUCTURED PROBLEMS TO BE SOLVED IN MANAGEMENT SYSTEMS

Management systems tackle, in particular, problems which are classified as complex ill-structured.

A problem is ill-structured if in its description [1]:
- qualitative features prevail;
- the representation is implicit;
- the quantities are not specified or determined in advance.

A problem is complex if the indices of the following characteristics of its description are high [2].
- dimension;
- non-linearity;
- stochasticity;
- dynamism;
- interdependence.

This kind of description of complex ill-structured problems places high demands on the problem-solver for their solution. Therefore computers may be of considerable help to the problem-solver. Because the problem is ill-structured, however, computers cannot in principle replace the creative, or intellectual, component of the problem-solver's activity and so he retains his dominating position. For this reason interactive systems are needed. Their effectiveness is largely dependent on the degree to which they adapt to the actual behaviour of the problem-solver. Thence follows the need to study the behaviour of experienced and skilled problem-solvers and to design descriptive models of their behaviour [3].

The writers have developed such models to solve three complex ill-structured problems to be tackled in management systems. They are object ordering [4], resource allocation [5] and planning [6]. The descriptive models form the cores of the DISIOR, DISIOR-RESOURCE and DISIOR-SPEKTR interactive systems. What follows are the fundamentals for designing the DISIOR-RESOURCE system.

2. RESOURCE ALLOCATION AS A COMPLEX ILL-STRUCTURED PROBLEM

Resource allocation is a major planning task encountered in management systems and is investigated in operations research. It can be stated in the following way:

A set of objects are regarded which are characterized in terms of a totality of features which dictate both the system state and possible control. The latter kind of features will be referred to as resources. There are certain relations between the features of the system state and resources. An objective function is specified for a set of system features which are related by certain constraints. The function is required to establish a control, or to allocate the resources among the objects, so as to enable the objective function to take on extreme values.

In management systems this class of problems includes funding, supply and other activities.

The basic specifics of such problems in real life are:

(2.1) - the number of objects between which the resources are allocated is fixed;

(2.2) - the number of types of resource is fixed;

(2.3) - the amount to be allocated is limited;

(2.4) - the number of features which characterize the objects is high and not fixed in advance;

(2.5) - the scales of object feature measurements can be either quantitative or qualitative;

(2.6) - in a general case each object is regarded as a combination of its components which can be conditionally referred to as object "activity kinds";

(2.7) - the number of activity kinds varies from object to object and is generally high and not fixed in advance;

(2.8) - the number of features which characterize an activity kind may be low but not fixed in advance;

(2.9) - the objective function is the implicit problem-solver's system of preferences, which is of complex nature in a general case;

(2.10)- the features which characterize the objects and activity kinds differ in importance in the problem-solver's system of preferences;

(2.11)- the resources to be allocated between objects and activity kinds can be interrelated in a general case;

(2.12)- the resource allocation process is a multi-stage procedure;

(2.13)- at each stage of the procedure the problem-solver either allocate the resources or establishes the relations between them for objects and activity kinds or their combinations;

(2.14) - resource allocation for certain objects and activity kinds can repeat itself in certain combinations at different stages of the procedure;

(2.15) - the more (or the less) preferable the objects or activity kinds from the problem-solver's point of view, the more obvious to the problem-solver are the rules for allocation of the resources between them.

3. A DESCRIPTIVE MODEL OF A PROBLEM-SOLVER'S BEHAVIOUR IN RESOURCE ALLOCATION

A major concept used in the design of descriptive models is "bounded rationality" [7] whereby the problem-solver only partly perceives the problem he faces. When the problem exceeds his capability, he replaces it with a simplified model which retains the basic properties of the problem and so enables him to stay within the framework of "rationality", or logically motivated behaviour, in its solution.

The descriptive models of the problem-solver's behaviour reported in the literature include elements of description of various aspects of his behaviour, in particular, in the development of decision rules.

It would be useful, however, to design such a model of the entire problem-solving process.

The designing such a model we made use of the findings obtained by analysing an actual problem-solver's behaviour, in particular, the responses made by experienced, highly skilled problem-solvers to a questionnaire and the experimental data and conclusions reported in the literature. As a result, a number of assumptions were made about a problem-solver's behaviour which are represented in the set-theoretic language as rules of his behaviour. The set of rules makes it possible to describe the behaviour of a problem-solver on the whole when solving the problem of resource allocation as a certain solution procedure. Note that this may be regarded as a possible description of the complex process which the problem-solver's behaviour constitutes.

In the descriptive model the number of objects o between which the resources f should be allocated is finite and fixed. This is also true of the number of resource types. Each object is regarded as a totality of its components which are object activity kinds c, whose number varies with the object and is in general high and not fixed in advance. The number of criteria k, the estimates of which give the problem-solver a clue as to how the resources should be allocated, may be high and not fixed in advance. The solution procedure takes many stages. At each i-th stage the problem-solver regards the following sets as initial information: of objects O; of their activity kind C; of features which characterize the object activity kinds K; of resources to be allocated F. The features of object activity kinds can be expressed, depending on the degree of their generalization, as sign systems of various levels, $K \sqsubset K^u \sqcup K^v \sqcup K^w$ where K^u, K^v and K^w are information about activity kinds in the form of opinions of the values or ranges of features, the presence or absence of features, and the presence or absence of generalized indices, or "names" [4].

The problem-solver determines the solution method which is associated with a set of criteria - features K_Σ the number of which is in general high and not fixed in advance. From the set of the criteria of the solution method the problem-solver identifies the most important set of criteria K_I, the number of which is not high and is fixed and the associated scale of measurements.

Using the most important totality of criteria K_I the problem-solver generates, wherever possible, the extreme regions of clearly more or less preferable values $(E_{I\hat{+}} \sqcup E_{I\hat{-}}) \sqsubset E_I$ on the set of measurement scale values E_I. If this is impossible, the problem-solver proceeds to consider the set of feature estimates for the activity kinds E_{I*} and generates on that set, wherever possible, the extreme regions of clearly more or less preferable estimates $(E_{I*\hat{+}} \sqcup E_{I*\hat{-}}) \sqsubset E_{I*}$. For most or least preferable activity kinds $(C_+ \sqcup C_-) \sqsubset C$, the estimates of which belong to extreme regions, the problem-solver usually has an idea of how to allocate the resources. He either directly allocates them or establishes relations on them. In solving the problem the problem-solver does not necessarily have an estimate of features for the activity kinds under consideration or, if an estimate is available, he cannot determine whether these activity kinds are the most or the least preferable. C_{ue} and C_{ur} denote sets of unestimated and unrelated activity kinds. If the sets C_{ue} and C_{ur} are non-empty or if the problem-solver cannot generate extreme regions or allocate resources to activity kinds, he returns to the start of the stage and changes the most important set of criteria or the solution method so as to resolve the situation at hand. Furthermore, the problem-solver may also resort to short cuts in order to obtain certain intermediate and final results of the stage. Consequently, the problem-solver comes to a solution of the initial problem in a finite number of stages.

In the solution process the problem-solver's activity may be regarded as filling out an objects - features - decision table, Fig. 1.

MAIN PART															
Objects	Object activity kind	Feature k			Inter-mediate decision Ψ			Final decision Φ							
o	c	k_1	k_2	...	Ψ_1	Ψ_2	...	f_1	Φ_1^1	Φ_2^1	...	f_k	Φ_1^k	Φ_2^k	...
	c_{10}														
	c_{11}														
	⋮														
o_1	c_{10}, c_{11}														
	c_{10}, c_{12}														
	⋮														
	c_{n0}														
	c_{n1}														
	⋮														
o_n	c_{n0}, c_{n1}														
	c_{n0}, c_{n2}														
	⋮														
$o_1, o_2,$	c_{10}, c_{20}														
$\dots o_n$	c_{10}, c_{30}														
	⋮														
AUXILIARY PART															
o	c	$\bar{k}$			$\bar{\Psi}$			$\bar{\Phi}$							
		$\bar{k}_1$	$\bar{k}_2$	...	$\bar{\Psi}_1$	$\bar{\Psi}_2$		f_1	$\bar{\Phi}_1^1$	$\bar{\Phi}_2^1$		f_k	$\bar{\Phi}_1^k$	$\bar{\Phi}_2^k$	

Fig. 1. Objects-features-decision table.

The columns of the Table are: objects o; object actitivy kinds c; features k; intermediate decision concerning resource allocation Ψ ; final decision concerning resource allocation Φ ; resources f. In the solution process the intermediate decisions help the problem-solver to reach final decisions and the latter decisions to achieve allocation.

The Table includes two parts, a main section and an auxiliary section. They are different in that the main part is completed by the problem-solver for specific object activity kinds whereas the auxiliary part is used by the problem-solver to deal with non-specific objects. Judgements on these, such as "for all objects ..." or "for all objects which feature the property ...", enable the problem-solver to complete the main part of the table.

Findings about the actual behaviour of the problem-solver obtained by means of a descriptive model were embodied in an interactive system which adapts to his actual behaviour.

4. AN INTERACTIVE DISIOR - RESOURCE SYSTEM WHICH INCORPORATES A DESCRIPTIVE PROBLEM SOLVER'S MODEL

In interactive systems computer sometimes play a dominant role. This is impossible, however, unless the problem can be easily formalized or is well-structured. In an ill-structured problem the computer's role is played by the problem-solver; the computer does not "replace" him, it rather "helps", or "serves" him. The computer supplies information, enhances the problem-solver's analytical abilities, provided that formal methods are applicable, and urges the problem-solver to exploit his creativity and use his experience and intuition.

The interactive DISIOR - RESOURCE system is intended to solve the resource allocation problem. The problem-solver maintains a dominant role; he stores the necessary information and employs a system of preferences. The computer organizes the solution procedure as a whole; it leaves the creative component to the problem-solver and takes over routine functions such as recording and storage of the information supplied by the problem-solver, display of intermediate and final decisions, etc.

The dialogue scenario is compiled with the use of elements from the descriptive model .

In a general case the dialogue is a multi-stage procedure, the general structure of which is the same at each stage. Each stage results in partial resource allocation among objects or their activity kinds. The solution procedure terminates if the resources are allocated to each object or if the problem-solver feels that there is no point in continuing.

The dialogue proceeds through a terminal. The problem-solver sees on the screen a sequence of questions, guidelines, and messages and responds to them by using the keyboard.

A dialogue scenario is made up of five types of modules:

i) Question;

ii) Directive;

iii) Variant;

iv) Preparation;

v) Comparison.

The Question module, which is denoted as MQ, is a question to be answered by the problem-solver. An answer is a choice and involves depression of a key for either Yes or No.

The Directive module, denoted MD, is a guideline for the problem-solver and consists of two components, in the order of their sequence:

(4.1) Directive, D

(4.2) Form to be filled, F.

In addition to a constant or fixed part, F includes a variable part which is made up of blanks to be filled out by the computer depending on the turn the solution process takes. Furthermore, some blanks should be filled by the problem-solver.

The problem-solver responds to the Directive module by filling out blanks in F from the terminal keyboard in following the instructions contained in the module.

The Variant module, denoted MV, is a set of variants of subsequent activities on the part of the problem-solver or information for him. He responds to this module by choosing and depressing the key of the terminal keyboard which contains the chosen variant number.

If in responding to Question, Directive or Variant module the problem-solver makes a mistake caused by violation of the instructions given in the module or of the general logic of the dialog scenario, information about the error is displayed. He should re-key his answer.

The Preparation module, which is denoted as MP, is a message for the problem-solver where either he is informed about results obtained at preceding stages or further steps in solving the problem are described.

In addition to the constant, or fixed, part MP also includes a variable part, which consists of blanks to be filled out by the computer in compliance with certain rules and depending on the course of the solution process.

The Comparison module, denoted MC, permits the modules to follow in different orders. In this module the computer checks certain conditions; the findings dictate transition to another module.

The aggregated blocks which combine into DISIOR-RESOURCE are shown in Fig. 2. Some of the blocks (1, 4, 10, 11, 12, 13, and 14) are intended for the programmer and researcher; others (2, 3, 5, 6, 7, 8, 9 and 15) are chiefly intended for the problem-solver. With some (2, 5, 6, 7, 8, 9, and 15) the problem-solver is obliged to work, with others (3, 5, and 15) he can do so only if he wishes; for this he summons them from the terminal.

DISIOR, DISIOR-RESOURCE and DISIOR-SPEKTR have been implemented in mini computer and large computer software and several programming languages, tested and will be used both for training managers and for the more effective solution of problems in planning and management.

5. NUMERICAL EXAMPLE

Further the separate stage of the explanatory example of DISIOR-RESOURCE program is shown. The example illustrates the solution process (with the use of DISIOR-RESOURCE) for the problem of financing some objects. The problem under consideration is complex and ill-structured.

Modules MQ, MD, MV and MP are enumerated according to their lists, the number being shown on the right of the module symbol. The numerical example starts with the second stage.

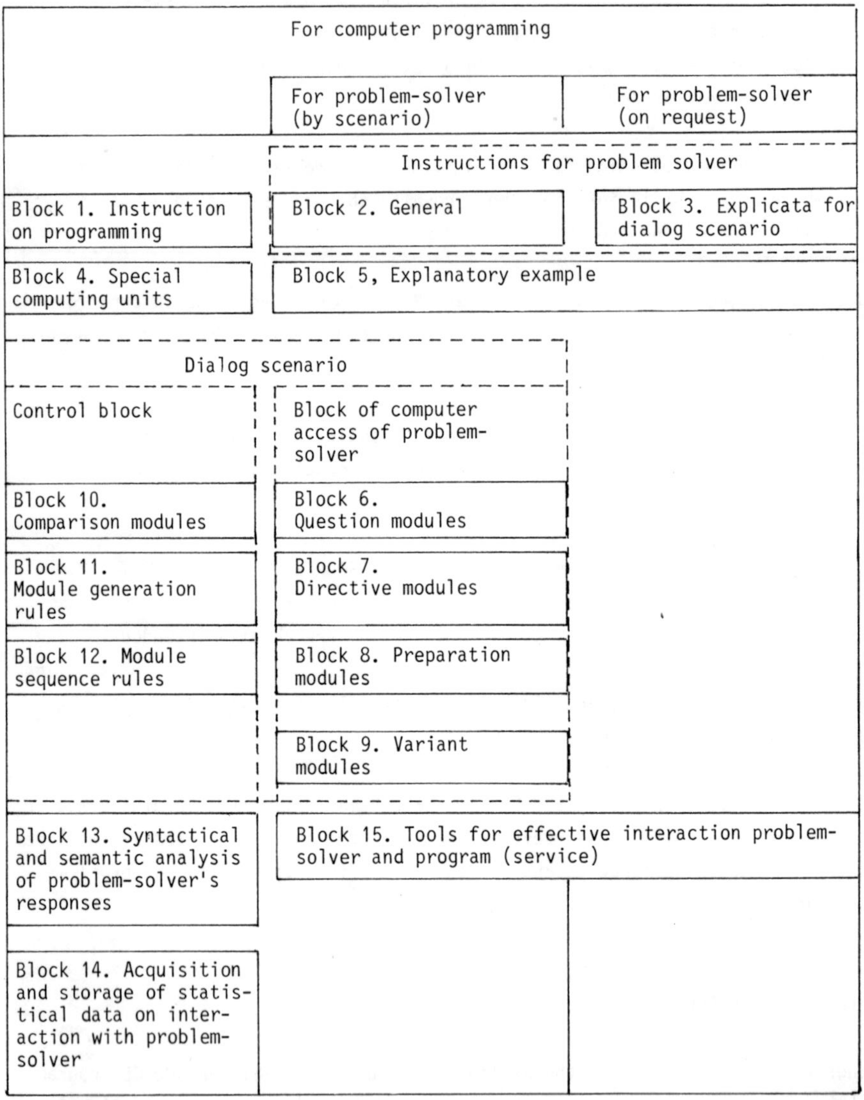
For computer programming
For problem-solver (by scenario)
For problem-solver (on request)
Instructions for problem solver
Block 1. Instruction on programming
Block 2. General
Block 3. Explicata for dialog scenario
Block 4. Special computing units
Block 5, Explanatory example
Dialog scenario
Control block
Block of computer access of problem-solver
Block 10. Comparison modules
Block 6. Question modules
Block 11. Module generation rules
Block 7. Directive modules
Block 12. Module sequence rules
Block 8. Preparation modules
Block 9. Variant modules
Block 13. Syntactical and semantic analysis of problem-solver's responses
Block 15. Tools for effective interaction problem-solver and program (service)
Block 14. Acquisition and storage of statistical data on interaction with problem-solver

Fig. 2. Components of DISIOR-RESOURCE program

MP 9. Stage 2.

The further steps are connected with the selection of o, c, f for this stage.

MD 9. Type objects o.

Response: o_1, o_2, o_3, o_4, o_5, o_6.

MD 10. Type object activities c.

Response: c_{10}, c_{20}, c_{30}, c_{40}, c_{50}, c_{60}. *)

MD 11. Type resources f.

Response: f_1. **)

MQ 3. Do you need the previous information about o, c, f?

Response: No.

MV 2. There are variants of activities to choose:

1) to type $\Psi, \Phi, \bar{\Psi}, \bar{\Phi}$;
2) to type E_{extr*}, E_{extr}; ***)
3) to type K_I;
4) to end this stage and to go to the next one.

Response: 1.

MV 13. There are variants of decision records to choose:

1) main part of the table: Ψ, Φ;
2) auxiliary part of the table: $\bar{\Psi}, \bar{\Phi}$;
3) auxiliary and main parts of the table: $\bar{\Psi}, \bar{\Phi}, \Psi, \Phi$.

Response: 2.

MP 24. The further steps are connected with records of $\bar{\Psi}, \bar{\Phi}$.

MV 14. There are variants of decision records for the auxiliary part of the table to choose:

1) $\bar{\Phi}$;
2) $\bar{\Psi}$;
3) $\bar{\Psi}, \bar{\Phi}$.

Response: 1.

---

*) - c_{io} coincides with o_i, i.e. $c_{io} = o_i$.

**) - f_1 means the single resource to allocate - finance.

***) - E_{extr*}, E_{extr} mean respectively $E_{I*\hat{+}} \sqcup E_{I*\hat{-}}$, $E_{I\hat{+}} \sqcup E_{I\hat{-}}$.

MD 36. Type $\bar{\Phi}(f)$.

Response: For any object o: $0{,}9\ k_1 \leq f_1(o) \leq 1{,}2\ k_1$. *)

MD 40. Type K_I.

Response: k_1.

MD 43. Type the estimates e of k_1 for c.

Response: $e(c_{10}) = 120$;
$e(c_{20}) = 180$;
$e(c_{30}) = 200$;
$e(c_{40}) = 80$;
$e(c_{50}) = 150$;
$e(c_{60}) = 220$.

MD 26. Type $\Phi(f)$.

Response: $c_{10} : 108 \leq f_1(c_{10}) \leq 144$;
$c_{20} : 162 \leq f_1(c_{20}) \leq 216$;
$c_{30} : 180 \leq f_1(c_{30}) \leq 240$;
$c_{40} : 72 \leq f_1(c_{40}) \leq 96$;
$c_{50} : 135 \leq f_1(c_{50}) \leq 180$;
$c_{60} : 192 \leq f_1(c_{60}) \leq 264$.

MP 19. The information about all previous $\Phi(f)$ for c:

$$c_{10} + c_{20} + c_{40} + c_{50} + c_{60} : f_1(c_{10}) + f_1(c_{20}) + f_1(c_{30}) + f_1(c_{40}) + f_1(c_{50}) + f_1(c_{60}) = 1000;$$

$c_{10} : 108 \leq f_1(c_{10}) \leq 144$;
$c_{20} : 162 \leq f_1(c_{20}) \leq 216$;
$c_{30} : 180 \leq f_1(c_{30}) \leq 240$;
$c_{40} : 72 \leq f_1(c_{40}) \leq 96$;
$c_{50} : 135 \leq f_1(c_{50}) \leq 180$;
$c_{60} : 192 \leq f_1(c_{60}) \leq 264$. **)

MQ 11. Can you allocate f for o?

Response: No.

MV 11. There are variants of activities to choose:

1) to go to the next stage;
2) to change K_I.

Response: 1.

---

*) - the problem solver forms $\Phi(f)$ using the criterion k_1 mentioned by him at the first stage.

**) - the computer represents the information about finance allocations obtained by the problem solver at all previous stages.

The problem solver goes to the next stage. After some stages the solution process results in the finance allocation among the objects.

CONCLUSIONS

Complex ill-structured problems faced by management systems were discussed.

For solution of three such problems, namely, object ordering, resource allocation and planning, descriptive models of problem solver's behaviour led to interactive systems DISIOR, DISIOR-RESOURCE and DISIOR-SPEKTR respectively, which adapt to the actual behaviour of the problem-solver. DISIOR, DISIOR RESOURCE and DISIOR-SPEKTR have been implemented in various computers and several programming languages; they will be used both for training managers and for the more effective solution of problems in planning and management.

The systems have been updated to incorporate additional knowledge of problem-solvers behaviour obtained in system testing.

6. REFERENCES

1 Simon, H.A. Information-processing theory of human problem solving. - Handbook of learning and cognitive processes. Ed. by W.K. Estes, v. 5, Human information processing, 1978, p. 271-295.

2 Naylor, T.N. Computer simulation experiments with models of economic systems, Wiley & Sons, Inc. N.Y. , 1971.

3 Tuggle, F.D. - F.H. Barron On the validation of descriptive theories of human decision-making. 7-th research conference on subjective probability, utility and decision-making, Goteborg, Sweden, 1979.

4 Khaynish, S.V. - A.G. Vlasov A Descriptive approach to Simulation of Decision Maker's Behaviour in Management Systems. Problemy MSNTI, Moscow, MTsNTI, 1979, No 1, pp. 41-78.

5	Vlasov, A.G. - S.V. Khaynish	A Descriptive Approach to Simulation of Man's Behaviour in Making a Decision on Resource Allocation (preprint). MNIIPU, Moscow, 1980.
6	Yermakova, A.V. - S.V. Khaynish - L.N. Tsyganokov	An algorithm for solution of a complex ill-structured management problem (with reference to planning information publications on geological surveying). Algorithms and programs / All-Union Research Institute of Mineral Raw Material Economics and Geological Surveying. Sectoral Fund of Algorithms and Programs "Geology", Issue 6(47), Moscow, 1981.
7	March, J.G. - H.A. Simon	Organizations, John Wily & Sons, New York, 1964.

THEORY AND PRACTICE OF
MULTIPLE CRITERIA DECISION MAKING
C. Carlsson and Y. Kochetkov (editors)

MULTICRITERIA PROBLEMS IN POOLING RESOURCES

E.E. DUDNIKOV, V.S. MOLOSTVOV
International Research Institute of Management Sciences
Schepkina Street 8, 129090 Moscow USSR

ABSTRACT

The paper is concerned with optimization models for establishing the contributions made by several interested parties to supplies of various resources for certain joint projects. The models are intended for computing compromise versions of allocating the shares among the parties and employing information about the potential and preferences of the contributors.

The models are formalized as a series of multi-criteria (linear) programming problems. Several principles determining a decision are suggested. The characteristic decisions from a set of Pareto optima are identified which correspond to certain meaningful verbal formulations (uniform minimization of costs sustained by the contributors, equal benefits, etc.). In computing such solutions a certain tentative allocation is used as is information on various "utopian" values of objective functions which cannot be attained simultaneously. The proposed approach relies on linear programming. The models are implemented as interconnected FORTRAN-4 programs which can be operated either in batches or interactively.

These models are used for studies of pooling (through long-term multilateral crediting) material, finance, labour and other resources in joint large-scale CMEA construction projects.

1. INTRODUCTION

This article will describe optimization models for determining the size of contributions made by a number of interested parties to a pool of resources for joint activities. The models are intended for computing compromise versions of the amounts to be supplied by the parties and rely on information about the potential and preferences of the parties. They are formalized as a series of multicriteria programming problems. The linear version of the models is implemented in FORTRAN-4 programs which can be used in batch or interactive modes.

These models are applied to the problem of pooling (through long-term multilateral crediting) material, technical, finance, labour and other resources in large-scale construction projects by CMEA member nations. These projects may cost thousands of millions of roubles and assigning the shares to be contributed by each party concerned is a major step towards reaching an agreement on joint construction. An informal description of this problem, linear models, and the results of model computations have been presented in ref. [1]

2. STATEMENT OF THE PROBLEM

For several parties to carry out a joint project they have to allocate N kinds of resources in amounts $R^1, \ldots, R^N$ respectively. A resource is treated broadly as "anything needed for the project to materialize".

Hereafter the subscript i denotes the number of the resource ($i = 1, \ldots, N$) and the subscript j, the number of the party ($j = 1, \ldots, M$); summation over i is carried out from 1 to N and over j from 1 to M.

The following notation is used:

x_j^i - the amount of the i-th resource to be supplied by the j-th party;

$x^i = (x_1^i, \ldots, x_M^i)$ - the distribution of supplies of the i-th resource among the parties;

$x_j = (x_j^1, \ldots, x_j^N)$ - the vector of supplies by the j-th party;

$C = (c^1, \ldots, c^N)$ - the vector of resource prices.

The variables x_j^i should satisfy N conditions of equilibrium

$$\sum_j x_j^i = R^i \quad (i = 1, \ldots, N) \tag{1'}$$

or, in the vectorial form,

$$\sum_j x_j = R. \tag{1}$$

The contribution of the j-th party is measured as*)

$$c \quad x_j = G_j \tag{2}$$

which will be referred to as the size of his credit.

Legal, commercial and other forms of and rules for sharing in the project and in the payment and distribution of profits may be extremely varied. They are, however, assumed to be coordinated and agreed upon so that all the benefits which the j-th party is to obtain from the project following its materialization are a function of its credit size B_j and independent of the specific set of resources x_j which ensures the credit.

The quantity $q_j = B_j / \sum_j B_j$ will be referred to as the share of the j-th party in the resources of the project (it is obvious that $\sum_j q_j = 1$) and the total price of the necessary resoursces $S = c \cdot R$ as the project cost. From condition (1) it follows that $S = \sum_j c \quad x_j = \sum_j B_j$ and from (2) and definition of q_j it follows that $c \quad x_j = B_j = q_j S$.

To begin with, let us assume that the shares q_i are agreed on. Then, in condition (2) $B_j = q_j S = \text{const}$, or the cost of supply by the j-th party in the prices c is a given quantity. Even in this case a party is not indifferent to the set of resources constituting his contribution, B_j, because the conditions for manufacture, stocks, and economic value of a unit of the same resource may differ from one party to another. Therefore the following problem should be solved:

With specified shares it is required to find such balanced (or satisfying conditions (1) and (2)) versions of the distribution of resource supplies among the parties that would recognize their preferences about the kind of resources which constitute their credits.

*) $a \cdot b = \sum_K a_K b_K$ denotes a scalar product of vectors a and b.

Let X_j be a set of possible supplies by the j-th party which is dependent on technological and economic constraints, the possibilities of replacement and the completion of certain resources and also on condition (2). Let X denote the set of all admissible distributions $x = (x_1, \ldots, x_M)$ for which $x_j \in X_j$ $(j = 1, \ldots, M)$ and the equilibrium conditions (1) are met.

Let us assume that the preference system of each party is described by its objective function (criterion) $I_j(x_j)$, which is defined on the set X_j. Let us interpret $I_j(x_j)$ as an estimate made by the j-th party of its costs for supplying a set of resources x_j. Consequently, it wishes to minimize that cost function. The functions $I_j(x_j)$ are assumed to be continuous and increasing for each variable.

Let us introduce a vectorial objective function $I(x) = (I_1(x_1), \ldots, I_M(x_M))$ in a domain of definition $X \subset X_1 \times \ldots \times X_M$. In compliance with the ideas of theory of multicriteria decision-making [2, 3] it would be helpful to regard as solutions to the above problem only those versions of supply distributions which are Pareto-optimal in the multicriteria optimization problem

$$I(x) \to \min_{x \in X} . \tag{3}$$

3. CHOICE OF A SOLUTION FROM A SET OF PARETO-OPTIMA

It will be remembered that for any vector $\lambda = (\lambda_1, \ldots, \lambda_M)$ with positive components (weighting coefficients) $\lambda_j > 0$ a solution of the (single-criterion) minimization problem

$$\lambda \cdot I(x) = \sum_j \lambda_j I_j(x_j) \to \min_{x \in X} \tag{4}$$

is a (Pareto-optimal) solution of problem (3). On the other hand, if an additional condition of convexity of the functions I_j and sets X_j is imposed, each solution of problem (3) is a solution of problem (4) for certain non-negative weights $\lambda_1, \ldots, \lambda_M (\lambda \neq 0)$. In a linear case, important in applications, where the functions I_j are linear and X_j are polyhedra, the following necessary and sufficient conditions for Pareto-optimality hold:

---

x* is a Pareto-optimal solution of the problem (3) iff

x^* is a solution of the problem (4) with a certain vector $\lambda = (\lambda_1, \ldots, \lambda_M)$ with positive components.

The unique solution of multicriteria optimization problems is chosen on the basis of additional, often informal, considerations. Computation of the entire set of Pareto optima and, a point which is at least equally important, an illustrative presentation of this set to the decision-maker is found to be difficult with large M (starting with M = 4). Therefore in real life the reasoning about the way in which a final decision is made is often formulated in terms of weighting coefficients λ_j. This approach, with all its simplicity, has numerous disadvantages. In particular, in many cases there is no basis for choosing the values for weighting coefficients.

Another way is to establish additional conditions to be satisfied by final decisions. In doing so, information about certain characteristic (admissible or inadmissible) points x and associated values of I(x) may be used. This approach is used in this paper. Certain reference points are employed such as "utopian" points and "status" points.

Let $\mathring{x} = (\mathring{x}_1, \ldots, \mathring{x}_M)$ be an initial supply distribution which has been tentatively agreed. This, for instance, may be the following "fair" proportional distribution, $\mathring{x}_j = q_j R$. The initial distribution is associated with the "status" point $\mathring{I} = I(\mathring{x}) = (I_1(\mathring{x}_1), \ldots, I_M(\mathring{x}_M))$ in the criterion space $\mathbb{R}^N$. It is desirable to proceed from this distribution (which is not Pareto-optimal, generally speaking) to a new distribution from the set of Pareto-optima. In doing so information can be used about certain unattainable, "utopian" points I, for which there is no $x \in X$ such that $I(x) = \check{I}$ (or $I(x) \leq \check{I}$) but which characterize the utmost potential for minimizing the parties' costs.

Let us have a closer look at three cases

$$\check{I}_j = \check{I}_j(1) = \min_{x_j \in X_j} I_j(x_j) \qquad (j = 1, \ldots, M), \tag{5}$$

$$\check{I}_j = \check{I}_j(2) = \min_{x \in X} I_j(x_j) \qquad (j = 1, \ldots, M), \tag{6}$$

$$\check{I}_j = \check{I}_j(3) = \min_{\substack{x \in X \\ I(x) \leq \mathring{I}}} I_j(x_j) \qquad (j = 1, \ldots, M). \tag{7}$$

In the j-th problem of case (5) a solution to the supply problem is found which best suits the j-th party. Since this is done taking into account only its own constraints, $x_j \in X_j$, the resultant supply solutions $x_1(1), \ldots, x_M(1)$ are not balanced (condition (1) is not met). In the j-th problem of case (6) an acceptable (balanced) solution satisfying all parties is found which is the most beneficial for the j-th party. With this distribution $x(2,j)$ the other parties' costs, $I_K(x_K(2, j)) = I_K(2, j)$ $(K \neq j)$, can exceed their expenses $\mathring{I}_K$ with the initial distribution. In the j-th problem of case (7) this possibility is eliminated since only those distributions $x \in X$ are considered which are at least as good as the initial one. The solution of the j-th problem in (7) is denoted as $x(3, j)$ and $I_K(3, j) = I_K(x_K(3, j))$ $(K = 1, \ldots, M)$.

Problems (5) - (7) are concerned with utmost potential for reducing the parties' costs. They generate "utopian" points, I(1), I(2) and I(3), which can be helpful in determining the overall balanced distribution $x \in X$. A formalization and interpretation in meaningful terms of this approach are given below.

Consider a mathematical programming problem

$$\gamma^* = \max_{\substack{x \in X \\ I_j(x_j) \leq (1-\gamma_j \gamma)\mathring{I}_j \\ (j=1, \ldots, M)}} \gamma \tag{8}$$

where $\gamma_1, \ldots, \gamma_M$ are non-negative coefficients.

With $\gamma_1 = \ldots = \gamma_M = 1$ a solution, $x(4)$, of problem (8) is a distribution which reduces each party's costs in comparison with version $\mathring{x}$ by at least $100\gamma^*\%$, γ^* being the maximum possible value of γ which exhibits this property. In a general case where γ_j are not equal, solution $x(4)$ ensures that the costs are reduced by at least $100\gamma_j\gamma^*\%$ for the j-th party. The coefficients γ_j can be specified in different ways, for example,

$$\gamma_j = \gamma_j^0 \quad \text{are specified exogenously} \tag{9}$$

$$\gamma_j^1 = \frac{\mathring{I}_j - I_j(1,j)}{\mathring{I}_j} = \frac{\mathring{I}_j - \check{I}_j(1)}{\mathring{I}_j}, \tag{10}$$

$$\gamma_j^2 = \frac{\mathring{I}_j - I_j(2,j)}{\mathring{I}_j} = \frac{\mathring{I}_j - \check{I}_j(2)}{\mathring{I}_j}, \tag{11}$$

$$\gamma_j^3 = \frac{\mathring{I}_j - I_j(3,j)}{\mathring{I}_j} = \frac{\mathring{I}_j - \check{I}_j(3)}{\mathring{I}_j} . \tag{12}$$

The values, $100\gamma_j^1$, $100\gamma_j^2$ and $100\gamma_j^3$, are cost reduction percentages for the j-th party in proceeding from the distribution $\mathring{x}_j$ to solutions of problems (5), (6) and (7) respectively. These values cannot be obtained simultaneously in the same distribution $x \varepsilon X$ because they are obtained with different distributions. The use of γ_j^l as γ_j in problem (8) results in balanced distributions which yield the maximum possible percentage of the largest possible cost reductions for the parties $(\mathring{I}_j - \check{I}_j(l))$ (l = 1,2,3). To be more specific, the distribution which is obtained by solving the problem (8) with $\gamma_j = \mathring{\gamma}_j$ or $\gamma_j = \gamma_j^1$ reduces the costs for the j-th party by at least $100\gamma_j\gamma^*\%$ (for some parties by exactly this amount). With $\gamma_j = \gamma_j^l$ (l = 2, 3) in the convex case, the resultant distribution leads to a percentage $(100\gamma^*\%)$, which is the maximum possible cost $(\mathring{I}_j - \check{I}_j(l))$ for all the parties. In all cases γ^* is the maximum possible value of γ which features this property.

Problem (8) has a simple geometrical interpretation, see Fig. 1. Let us denote $I(X) = \{ I = (I_1, \ldots, I_M) \mid I = I(x), x \varepsilon X \}$ and let $I(X_\gamma)$ denote a subset of $I(X)$ which is dictated by the constraints of problem (8). Note that in a linear case $I(X)$ and $I(X_\gamma)$ are bounded polyhedra. Let γ_j be represented as $\gamma_j = \gamma_j^l$ (l = 1,2,3) (see (10) - (12)). Let $[\mathring{I}, \check{I}(l)]$ be a segment of the straight line between the "status" point and the l-th "utopian" point. Let this segment be represented in a parametric form

$$I(\gamma) = \mathring{I} + \gamma(\check{I}(l) - \mathring{I}), \ \gamma \varepsilon [0, 1] . \tag{13}$$

The subset $I(X_\gamma)$ is easily seen to be an intersection of the sets $I(X)$ and $P^\gamma = \{I = (I_1, \ldots, I_M) \mid I_j \leq (1 - \gamma_j\gamma)\mathring{I}_j, \ j = 1, \ldots, M\}$. The set P^γ is obtained by a parallel shift of the non-positive orthant $\mathbb{R}_-^M = \{I \mid I_j \leq 0, \ j = 1, \ldots, M\}$; the apex of the shifted orthant P^γ is a point I^γ with coordinates $I_j^\gamma = (1 - \gamma_j\gamma)\mathring{I}_j$ (j = 1,..., M). Since it was assumed that $\gamma_j = \gamma_j^l$ (l = 1,2,3), this means in the light of (10) - (12), that

$$I_j^\gamma = \mathring{I}_j + \gamma(\check{I}_j(l) - \mathring{I}_j) = I_j(\gamma). \tag{14}$$

Consequently, the apex, $I^\gamma = I(\gamma)$, of the orthant P^γ stays on the segment $[\mathring{I}, \check{I}(l)]$ and, with γ varying from 0 to 1, the point I moves along this segment from $\mathring{I}$ to $\check{I}(l)$. The value $\gamma = \gamma^*$ represents the "extreme" position of the orthant P^γ in which the intersection $I(X) \cap P^\gamma = I(X_\gamma$ is non-empty and all

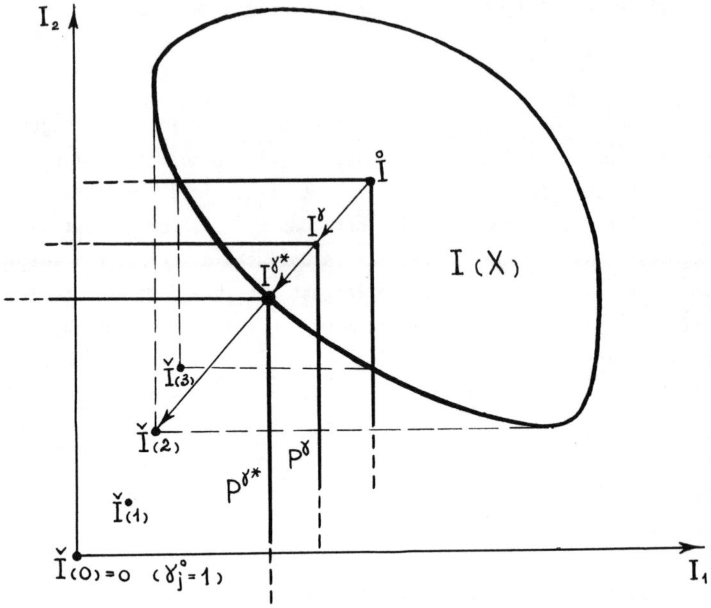

I_2
$\mathring{I}$
I^γ
$I^{\gamma*}$
$I(X)$
$\check{I}_{(3)}$
$\check{I}_{(2)}$
P^γ
$P^{\gamma*}$
$\check{I}_{(1)}$
$\check{I}_{(0)}=0$ $(\gamma_j^\circ=1)$
I_1

Fig. 1

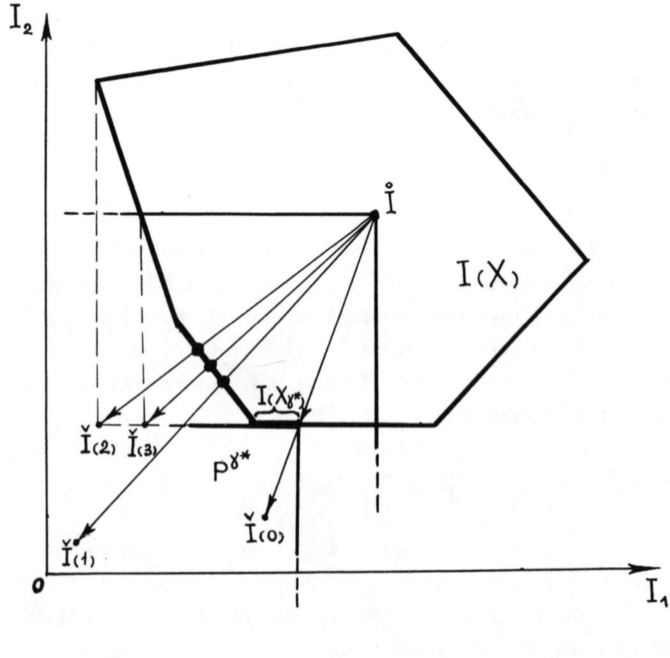

I_2
$\mathring{I}$
$I(X)$
$I(X_{\gamma*})$
$\check{I}_{(2)}$ $\check{I}_{(3)}$
$P^{\gamma*}$
$\check{I}_{(0)}$
$\check{I}_{(1)}$
0
I_1

Fig. 2

the points of the associated set $X_{\gamma *}$ are solutions to problem (8).

From this interpretation it is obvious that with the choice $\gamma_j = \gamma_j^1$ (1 = 1,3,3) any solution $x^* = x(4)$ cannot be improved upon simultaneously in terms of all the criteria or, alternatively, that there is no $\bar{x} \in X$ such that $I_j(\bar{x}) < I_j(x^*)$ for all $j = 1, \ldots, M$. Indeed, if $I(\bar{x}) < I(x^*)$, $x^* \in X$, then the point $I(\bar{x}) \in I(X)$ remains within the orthant P^{γ^*}. Consequently, the orthant P^{γ} can be moved "farther" along the segment $[\mathring{I}, \check{I}(1)]$ so that the point $I(\bar{x})$ lies on the boundary of the orthant P^{γ} with $\gamma > \gamma^*$. This, however, is inconsistent with the definition of γ^* (see (8)).

Let the coefficients $\gamma_j = \gamma_j^{\circ}$ be specified a priori. A "utopian" point $\check{I}(0)$ is introduced artificially with coordinates $\check{I}_j(0) = (1 - \gamma_j^{\circ})\, \mathring{I}_j$ $(j = 1, \ldots, M)$; this corresponds to the desire to reduce the costs of the j-th party by $100\gamma_j^{\circ}$%. Then γ_j° can be represented in the same form in which $\gamma_j^{1,2,3}$ was (see (10) - (12)

$$\gamma_j = \frac{I_j^{\circ} - \check{I}_j(0)}{\mathring{I}_j}$$

and an interpretation is possible similar to that given above using the segment $[\mathring{I}, \check{I}(0)]$. The non-improvability on the solution of problem (8) with $\gamma_j = \gamma_j^{\circ}$ is also retained. Care should be excercised in specifying the coefficients γ_j° a priori. It would be natural to introduce a condition $0 \leq \check{I}(0) \leq \mathring{I}$ from which it follows that $0 \leq \gamma_j^{\circ} \leq 1$. With γ_j specified, $x_j \in X_j$ does not necessarily exist such that $I_j(x_j) = \check{I}_j(0)$. In particular, this is the case if $\gamma_1 = \ldots = \gamma_M = 1$: because if so, then $I_j(0) = 0 \neq I_j(x_j) > 0$ with $x_j \in X_j$.

Thus, the solution $x^* = x(4)$ of problem (8) with $\gamma_j = \gamma_j^{0,1,2,3}$ cannot be improved upon over all I_j, or is said to be Slater-optimal. A more subtle question is whether it is Pareto-optimal? It will be remembered that the solution $x \in X$ is Pareto optimal iff there is no $\bar{x} \in X$ such that $I_j(\bar{x}_j) \leq I_j(x_j)$ with all $j = 1, \ldots, M$ and with at least one j the inequality is strict. For the solution $x^* = x(4)$ with $\gamma_j = \gamma_j^{0,1,2,3}$ the following properties hold: if I(X) is strictly convex then x^* is Pareto-optimal: if I(X) is non-convex, x^* is not necessarily Pareto-optimal (examples are available); if the set I(X) is convex (for example, a polyhedron), then the solution x^* is not necessarily Pareto-optimal (examples are available; see Fig. 2), in non-singular cases Pareto-optimality holds with $\gamma_j = \gamma_j^{2,3}$.

In the case of the Pareto-optimality of x^* the set $I(X_{\gamma^*})$ consists of a single point (but the solution x^* is not necessarily the only one possible). Note that the point $I(x^*)$ does not necessarily stay on the segment $[\overset{\circ}{I}, \check{I}\,(1)]$; in other words, some inequalities in the conditions of problem (8) in the point $x = x^*$ may hold as strict inequalities. In the convex non-singular case, however, with $\gamma_j = \gamma_j^{2,3}$ all these inequalities in the point x^* become equalities.

To sum up, this approach may be said to help in obtaining distributions which (i) are Pareto-optimal (or at least Slater-optimal) and (ii) satisfy the additional conditions formulated in terms of the initial costs $\overset{\circ}{I}_j$ and the desired values of costs $\check{I}_j$. In the convex case any of these distributions is certainly a solution of problem (8) with a certain vector of weighting coefficients $\lambda > 0$ $(\lambda \neq 0)$, but this vector is not known in advance.

4. EXAMPLE: LINEAR MODELS OF SHARING IN CONSTRUCTION PROJECTS

This approach has been used in modelling the pooling of resources for joint large-scale construction projects by CMEA member nations. The resources were building materials, construction machinery, the equipment to be installed following construction, labour, monetary funds, etc.

The j-th country is assumed to submit for the model the ranges of her possible supplies of each resource and other linear constraints $A_j x_j \leq d_j$ (technological, economic, etc.) where A_j is a constant matrix and d_j is a vector. The set X is described here in terms of linear individual constraints

$$X_j = \begin{cases} \sum_i c^i x_j^i = B_j \\ 0 \leq x_{j\,min}^i \leq x_j^i \leq x_{j\,max}^i \leq R^i \\ A_j x_j = d_j \end{cases} \qquad (j = 1, \ldots, M)$$

and total constraints

$$\sum_j x_j^i = R^i \quad (i = 1, \ldots, N).$$

The member countries wish to find supply distributions $x \in X$ which yield the smallest possible cost functions

$$I_j^B(x_j) = \sum_i \alpha_j^i x_j^i = \alpha_j x_j \qquad (15)$$

where α_j^i is an estimate made by the j-th country of her costs for the supply of a unit of the i-th resource. The countries are assumed to report their normalized estimates, or $\sum_i \alpha_j^i = 1$. The member countries are not required to supply information on the magnitude of costs. The quantities α_j^i act as coefficients of the "interchangeability" of resources in supplies by the j-th country as far as her costs are concerned.

An abridged version A and an expanded version C were developed as well as the basic model B for minimizing supply costs (15).

Version A does not use information about the coefficients α_j^i. The parties are only assumed to submit their wishes as to what resources they would like to supply in larger and what resources in smaller amounts (in comparison with $\mathring{x}_j$) and indicate the ranges of desired changes. The interests of the j-th country are modelled in this case as a function (to be maximized)

$$I_j^A(\mathring{x}_j) = \sum_i c^i \ | x_j^i - x_j^i |$$

which is the total cost of changes in the amounts to be shipped in compliance with the country's wishes. This function is actually linear.

In version C the shares q_i are assumed to be variable within ranges specified by the countries. The interests of the parties are represented as a "countribution efficiency" function (to be maximized)

$$I_j^C(x_j, \ q_j) = \beta_j S q_j - \sum_i \alpha_j^i \ x_j^i \qquad (16)$$

where α_j^i has been defined above and β_j is a coefficient which estimates the effect of the contribution $q_j S$ on the efficiency function. The first term in (16) is directly proportional to the size of the credit $B_j = q_j S$ of the j-th country, which will be repaid in the form of shipments of products from the plant to be constructed and the second term is an estimate of supply costs. Consequently, β_j denotes future benefits and supply costs. A more detailed interpretation of objective functions is given in ref. [1].

Shares to the pool are included in the parameters to be optimized and satisfy the constraints

$$0 \leq q_{j\ min} \leq q_j \leq g_{j\ max} \leq 1 \qquad (j = 1, \ldots, M)$$

(the condition $\sum_j q_j = 1$ is met automatically by virtue of (1) and (2)).

Note that in a general non-linear problem of resource pooling, the shares q_j may be the desired rather than fixed variables. The objective function of the j-th party is then dependent on the total size of the credit and the resources behind it: $I_j = \tilde{I}_j(q_j S,\ x_j) = I_j(q_j,\ x_j)$.

The structure of models of types A, B, and C, the information used and model outputs are summarized in Table 1.

For models of each type a scenario has been developed which is a sequence of interrelated submodels (tasks). Thus for a type B model it consists of six tasks associated with problems (5), (6), (7) and problem (8) with $\gamma_j = \gamma_j^{0,1,2,3}$ (see (9) - (12)) and problem (4). The outputs of some models are the inputs of others. Each task of the scenario is reducible to one or M linear programming problems. This also holds for the task associated with (8). The scenario for a type C model is written in a similar way; the scenario for a type A model contains only three tasks.

This set of models and tasks has been implemented as a set of interrelated Fortran-4 programs. Tasks are automatically converted into associated linear programming problems by service subroutines. The interactive mode enables the user to control the computation by correcting the data, choosing and changing the sequence of tasks, changing from one type of model to another, and regulating the amount of data to be displayed or printed.

The software for the models and model examples computed was developed by A.V. Likhachyov.

Experiments with models yielded certain qualitative findings; it was confirmed, in particular, that the larger the amount of information supplied by the user, the better the parties' interests are represented and the more effective the resultant solutions are. For details see ref. [1], in which are also discussed the dynamic versions of contributions to a pool.

The modelling results in a set of compromise Pareto- (or Slater-) optimal versions of resource supply distributions. These versions can be useful in drawing up actual agreements between the parties concerned.